KT-169-001

HIV in Primary Care

by

Dr Sara Madge, Dr Philippa Matthews,
Dr Surinder Singh and Dr Nick Theobald

MEDICAL FOUNDATION FOR AIDS & SEXUAL HEALTH*

*The Medical Foundation for AIDS & Sexual Health (MedFASH) is a charity supported by the British Medical Association. Registered charity no: 296689.

Published by

Medical Foundation for AIDS and Sexual Health
BMA House
Tavistock Square
London WC1H 9JP
© Medical Foundation for AIDS and Sexual Health 2004 (revised April 2005)

Acknowledgements

MedFASH is grateful for advice and comments from a wide range of individuals during the development of this booklet, including: Dr John Chisholm, Dr Andrew Dearden, Dr Stewart Drage, Dr Mustafa Kapasi and the British Medical Association (BMA)'s General Practitioners Committee; the Royal College of General Practitioners (RCGP) Sex, Drugs and HIV Task Group; Dr Patrick French, Professor Brian Gazzard, Professor George Kinghorn, Dr Martin Fisher, Professor Catherine Peckham, Dr Jean Tobin (for the BMA's Dermatology and Venereology Specialty Sub-Committee), and Ruth Webb. Thanks are also due to the following for help with drafting and information: Simon Crompton, Teresa Battison, Dr Deenan Pillay, Dr Pat Tookey, BMA Ethics Department, Stonewall and Dr Christopher Wilkinson.

The printing and dissemination of this booklet in England has been funded by the Department of Health. Development and design were made possible by the generous financial support of the BMA and by unrestricted grants from Abbott Laboratories, Bristol-Myers Squibb Pharmaceuticals Ltd, Boehringer Ingelheim Ltd, Gilead Sciences Ltd, GlaxoSmithKline, Merck Sharpe & Dohme Ltd, and Roche Products Ltd. MedFASH wishes to thank the West Midlands Deanery Postgraduate General Practice Education Unit for enabling Dr Philippa Matthews to contribute part of her time as an author.

Illustrations and figures are reproduced with the kind permission of Dr Adrian Mindel and Dr Melinda Tenant-Flowers (from ABC of AIDS), Dr MF Spittle (from ABC of AIDS), the Health Protection Agency, Medical Illustration UK Ltd, the Science Photo Library, the Wellcome Photo Library, the RCGP Sex, Drugs and HIV Task Group and the Primary Care Facilitation Team (Blood Borne Viruses) NHS Lothian.

Project management and editing: Ruth Lowbury, MedFASH executive director.
Project administration: Iain Webster, MedFASH administrator.
Editorial support and printing: BMA Publications Unit.
Design and layout: Hilary Tranter.

The authors are credited in alphabetical order.

The authors would like to thank Ruth Lowbury for the enormous amount of work she has put in to this booklet. It has benefited greatly from her thoroughness and eye for detail.

Cover

© CNRI/Science Photo Library
False colour transmission electron micrograph of human immunodeficiency virus particles inside a stricken T4 lymphocyte, a white blood cell of the immune system.

CONTENTS

CONTENTS

INTRODUCTION

About this booklet

The number of people with HIV infection continues to rise. There is no cure and no vaccine, although current treatments are life-saving. Around one third of those with HIV infection in the UK have yet to be diagnosed, even though many will be using primary care.

This booklet aims to provide essential information on HIV for GPs, practice nurses and other members of the primary healthcare team. The booklet provides:

- an update on HIV and the consequences of infection
- clear information on the clinical diagnosis of HIV in primary care
- information on HIV testing and prevention, and strategies for introducing them into primary care
- information on the management of people with HIV – with a primary care focus.

Comments about this booklet are welcome, and will inform future editions. Please send them to the Medical Foundation for AIDS & Sexual Health.

About the Medical Foundation for AIDS & Sexual Health (MedFASH)

MedFASH is a charity supported by the British Medical Association. It works with policy-makers and health professionals to promote excellence in the prevention and management of HIV and other sexually transmitted infections.

In 2003 MedFASH published *Recommended standards for NHS HIV services*, endorsed by the Department of Health and the British HIV Association. These were developed for England but are relevant for all parts of the UK.

Using the patient pathway as a framework, the standards address the role of both specialist and mainstream providers, highlighting the importance of managed service networks for consistent and equitable care delivery. The standards identify GPs and primary healthcare teams as playing an important part in the prevention and management of HIV, including diagnosis.

About the authors

Dr Sara Madge works as a GP in a north London practice and is an honorary senior lecturer in the Department of Primary Care at the Royal Free and University College Medical School, London. She is also an associate specialist at the Royal Free Centre for HIV Medicine having worked in HIV/AIDS for the past 12 years.

Dr Philippa Matthews is a general practitioner and GP trainer at Lee Bank Group Practice in Birmingham city centre. She also works in the West Midlands Deanery GP Unit as programme director for education in sexual health and HIV, commissioning and delivering education for primary care. She is an honorary senior lecturer at the University of Warwick. She has had an interest in HIV, sexual health and sexual history taking in primary care for many years.

Dr Surinder Singh is currently a general practitioner and clinical lecturer in general practice at the Royal Free and University College Medical School, London. He has worked in sexual health and HIV since 1987. He has been chairman of the Royal College of General Practitioners HIV working party and of the Lewisham PCT working group on sexual health and HIV. He is now a member of the Independent Advisory Group on Sexual Health. He works in a small but evolving practice in Deptford and New Cross, London. He is also an associate medical anthropologist at Brunel University, Middlesex.

Dr Nick Theobald trained in general practice in Bath and Wiltshire and was a GP principal in Swindon for nine years. He is currently associate specialist in HIV/genitourinary medicine at Chelsea and Westminster Hospital and Imperial College, London with responsibility for undergraduate and postgraduate education.

Foreword

This booklet is an important addition to practice libraries. Its contents are relevant to the work of all general practitioners, practice nurses and primary care teams.

Dr John
Chisholm CBE
Chairman,
General
Practitioners
Committee,
British Medical
Association
1997-2004

HIV continues to be one of the most important communicable diseases in the United Kingdom. It causes serious morbidity, significant mortality and the loss of high numbers of potential years of life, despite considerable advances in life-prolonging treatment that have led to a substantial reduction in the number of HIV-related deaths in the UK. Gratifyingly, HIV infection is now highly treatable. It is increasingly managed as a chronic disease, and many more patients survive for long periods. However, the costs of treatment and care remain high.

Currently, nearly fifty thousand people are infected with the human immunodeficiency virus in the UK. The numbers of those infected continue to rise fast, with a 20 per cent increase in new diagnoses between 2001 and 2002. Each year, many thousands of individuals are newly diagnosed as infected. Yet estimates suggest that almost a third of patients with HIV remain undiagnosed – many of whom will be using primary care. HIV-related morbidity and mortality are greater in those who are diagnosed late.

Whilst much of the treatment of HIV infection is specialised, general practice and primary care have important roles in helping infected patients. Increasingly, care will be delivered through partnership between specialised centres and primary care. This booklet gives considerable help and much useful and essential advice, as well as listing further sources of information. It deals with prevention, the clinical diagnosis of HIV infection in primary care, testing, and the management of infected people in primary care, including monitoring their adherence to treatment régimes. GPs and primary care teams can play important roles in the prevention, diagnosis and management of HIV infection, and in the care of the dying patient. Their potential involvement goes far beyond referral to specialist services.

This booklet will help general practitioners promote safer sexual practices, and assist them in giving advice to drug users, particularly if their practice has been commissioned to deliver an enhanced service for those patients. GPs are involved in screening pregnant women for HIV infection. GPs and practice nurses also need to be fully aware of what action to take when a needlestick injury has occurred, including seeking rapid expert advice about post-exposure prophylaxis.

General practice also provides opportunities to diagnose HIV infection, through clinical diagnosis when a patient presents with symptoms and signs that may suggest infection, and through offering diagnostic tests to those who are or may be at risk. This booklet is particularly helpful in suggesting ways of improving HIV detection, reminding GPs to be vigilant about the consequences of HIV infection – including opportunistic infections and malignancies – and in relation to those relatively common conditions that may signify underlying infection, and should prompt further enquiry, examination and assessment. (Throughout the text, urgent conditions and highly important information are clearly marked.) It is important to remember that people who are unaware they are infected are attending primary care. Early diagnosis can be lifesaving.

This booklet also explains when an HIV antibody test should be offered and gives helpful and detailed guidance about how to raise the subject, discussing risk, the other issues that might be covered in a pre-test discussion, and how to give the result.

Confidentiality, communication, continuity, sensitivity and a non-judgmental, non-discriminatory attitude are crucial components of the care of those who are or may be infected with HIV. The authors of this booklet give helpful advice, based on their own clinical practice, on the steps that can be taken to improve that care and to reinforce the trust between doctor and patient.

This booklet was initiated by the Medical Foundation for AIDS and Sexual Health whilst I was Chairman of the BMA's General Practitioners Committee. The GPC and the BMA continue to be strong supporters of the Foundation's work. I am pleased to have this opportunity to commend this excellent booklet to all GPs and primary care teams, and am confident it will prove both instructive and practical.

John Chisholm
29.9.2004

SECTION 1

HIV – core information

HIV – core information

For those who need an update on HIV, its effects and how it is treated and prevented

HIV in the UK: the figures
How common is HIV in the UK?

Human immunodeficiency virus (HIV) continues to be one of the most important communicable diseases in the UK, with 49,500 people thought to be infected at the end of 2002. Numbers are rising fast – there was a 20 per cent increase in new diagnoses between 2001 and 2002.

Of infections due to heterosexual transmission diagnosed in the UK, the majority were acquired abroad (see figure 3) and of these, most are attributable to exposure in sub-Saharan Africa.

The impact of treatment on death rates in the UK

Antiretroviral therapy (ART) and other interventions have resulted in a substantial reduction in the number of HIV-related deaths in the UK (see figure 1). Since the mid 1990s HIV has become a highly treatable condition.

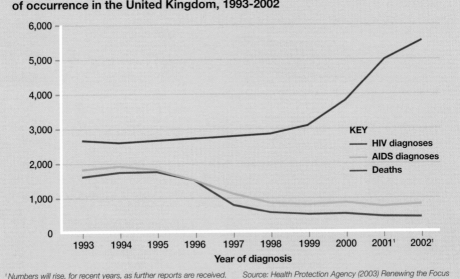

Figure 1. HIV & AIDS diagnoses and deaths in HIV-infected individuals by year of occurrence in the United Kingdom, 1993-2002

KEY
— HIV diagnoses
— AIDS diagnoses
— Deaths

Year of diagnosis

[1] Numbers will rise, for recent years, as further reports are received.   Source: Health Protection Agency (2003) Renewing the Focus

Figure 2: Number of new HIV diagnoses by year of diagnosis and probable route of exposure

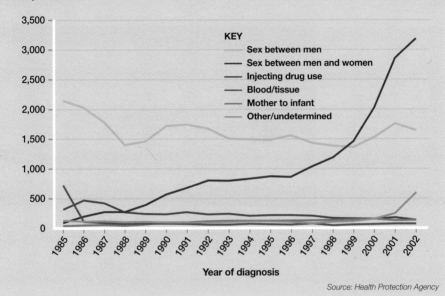

KEY
— Sex between men
— Sex between men and women
— Injecting drug use
— Blood/tissue
— Mother to infant
— Other/undetermined

Year of diagnosis

Source: Health Protection Agency

Figure 3: Heterosexually acquired infection by sub-category of heterosexual exposure

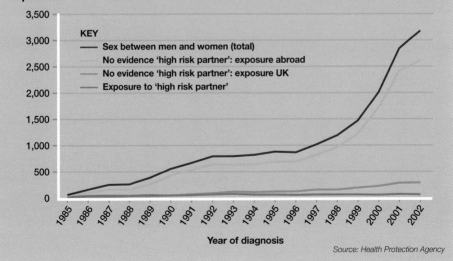

KEY
— Sex between men and women (total)
— No evidence 'high risk partner': exposure abroad
— No evidence 'high risk partner': exposure UK
— Exposure to 'high risk partner'

Year of diagnosis

Source: Health Protection Agency

SECTION 1

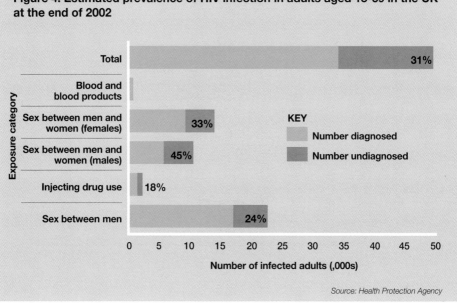

Figure 4: Estimated prevalence of HIV infection in adults aged 15-59 in the UK at the end of 2002

Exposure category

- Total: 31%
- Blood and blood products
- Sex between men and women (females): 33%
- Sex between men and women (males): 45%
- Injecting drug use: 18%
- Sex between men: 24%

KEY
- Number diagnosed
- Number undiagnosed

Number of infected adults (,000s)

Source: Health Protection Agency

Undiagnosed HIV

It is estimated that at the end of 2002 over 15,000 HIV-infected people remained undiagnosed – almost a third of the total infected (see figure 4). HIV-related morbidity and mortality are increasingly concentrated among those who are diagnosed late. Although many of these patients will do very well, treatment is more complex and it will take longer for satisfactory CD4 counts to be reached.

Monitoring HIV in the UK: how is it done?
Those known to have HIV

Figures for those known to have HIV derive from HIV treatment centres which give:

- numbers attending for care each quarter
- disease progression
- death rates.

Measuring undiagnosed HIV infection

The *Unlinked Anonymous Testing Programme* is a government-run programme established in 1990 to plot the trends of HIV infection in the community. Blood samples taken in participating centres for other reasons are tested for HIV on an anonymous basis. Information attached to the sample gives details such as age and whether the person is known to be infected with HIV. Sexual orientation is available for GUM clinic samples. However, no patient identifying details are linked to the sample, so positive results cannot be traced back.

For more detailed information The Health Protection Agency website www.hpa.org.uk has up-to-date figures for HIV, and slide sets that can be downloaded for teaching. These are best accessed by going to 'Infections Topics A-Z' then 'AIDS'.

Looking at trends in other infections

Transmission risks of hepatitis B and C and sexually transmitted infections (STIs) are closely linked with the risk of HIV transmission. Therefore, increases in these rates (especially within certain groups such as injecting drug users) might herald an increase in HIV transmission.

The virus and the natural history of HIV infection
The human immunodeficiency virus

HIV is a retrovirus which preferentially infects immune system cells – particularly CD4 cells (also known as T helper cells). It is always present in an infected person's blood. It is also present in other body fluids such as semen, vaginal secretions and breast milk.

In the first few weeks after infection with HIV there may be a flu-like illness (primary HIV infection or HIV seroconversion illness). Thereafter, the infected individual may be well (asymptomatic) for some years, although the virus is actively replicating. CD4 cells malfunction and die and the body attempts to keep replacing them. Ultimately the normal levels of CD4 cells can no longer be maintained and as their numbers decline the immune response is undermined. From the time of infection, it usually takes a number of years for the CD4 count to decline to levels which jeopardise immunity.

For more on symptoms of primary infection see p24

The consequences of HIV infection

If untreated, infection with HIV results in three groups of conditions:

Opportunistic infections (OIs)

Fungi, viruses, bacteria and other organisms that are usually harmless can all cause OIs. Some, such as herpes zoster, are simply commoner in the immunocompromised. Others, such as *pneumocystis* pneumonia (PCP, previously known as *pneumocystis carinii* pneumonia and, recently renamed *pneumocystis jiroveci*) only cause infection in the immunocompromised. People with HIV are more likely to develop symptoms and/or systemic infection with TB than those without HIV.

Malignancies

Some malignancies, such as lymphoma, Kaposi's sarcoma and carcinoma of the cervix, are commoner in HIV infected people.

For more on the clinical problems caused by HIV infection see p27

Direct effects

HIV itself causes a flu-like illness in the weeks after infection (see pages 24-26). In advanced disease it can also cause wasting, diarrhoea and neurological problems.

The Acquired Immune Deficiency Syndrome (AIDS)

AIDS was a term coined before the human immunodeficiency virus was identified in order to help classify and monitor this new medical condition. A patient was said to have AIDS when they developed certain conditions, such as specific opportunistic infections. There are now much better measures of disease advancement (see pages 15-17). The term AIDS now has limited value with respect to prognosis because of great improvements in treatment. It is still used as a category in epidemiological surveillance.

WELLCOME PHOTO LIBRARY

Herpes zoster. Commoner in those who are immunocompromised, this condition is one of the opportunistic infections associated with HIV.

Tests and clinical markers of HIV infection

HIV antibody test

This is the standard test for HIV. It is important to be aware that since HIV antibodies can take three months to develop after HIV infection (the window period), this test may miss HIV infection in the early stages. Therefore, the test may need to be repeated, depending on when infection may have occurred. The test gives no indication of disease progression.

Once a positive result has been found, blood is sent to a reference laboratory for final verification. Near patient tests are now available and their reliability is being explored in some community settings in the UK.

HIV p24 antigen

This test looks for evidence of HIV itself (as opposed to the antibody). It can be used to detect HIV in the window period (see HIV antibody test, above) if HIV seroconversion illness is suspected. It is best to arrange HIV antibody tests at the same time as p24 antigen, and again after the window period, for confirmation. Many laboratories now use tests which detect antibody and antigen in the same test, and are therefore optimal for early detection of infection.

If the individual is well, but concerned about very recent exposure to HIV (within 2 weeks) then the antibody or p24 antigen tests may still be negative: repeat testing will be required. Tests for HIV RNA are not currently recommended for primary care patients who may be recently infected with HIV because of a risk of false positive results.

CD4 count

Measuring the CD4 lymphocyte cell count is a useful indicator of the state of the immune system for those infected with HIV. The normal CD4 count

Table 1: How CD4 counts correlate with HIV-related problems

CD4 count cells/µL	Risk of opportunistic infection	Risk of HIV-associated tumours
> 500	Minimal or none	Very small increase in risk
500 – 200	Little risk unless falling rapidly, except TB	Small increase in risk
<200	Increased risk of serious opportunistic infection, eg: • *pneumocystis* pneumonia (PCP) • toxoplasmosis • oesophageal candida	Increasing risk
<100	Additional risk of • *mycobacterium avium intracellulare* • cytomegalovirus	High risk, and increasingly aggressive disease

is usually above 500 cells/μL. It is normal for CD4 counts to be quite variable – for example, if someone has a cold or recently had an immunisation. Therefore trends are more important than single readings. A patient with a CD4 count below 100 cells/μL is likely to have had immunodeficiency problems, but it is not inevitable that they are significantly unwell.

The CD4 count is an essential clinical tool in deciding whether antiretroviral therapy (ART) should be started, and when to prescribe prophylaxis against certain opportunistic infections.

Viral load

This is a measure of the amount of HIV in the blood. The higher the value the more active the virus and hence the disease process. A rising viral load shows that the virus is replicating at a higher rate. The viral load should fall

Figure 5. Association between virological, immunological, and clinical events and time course of HIV infection

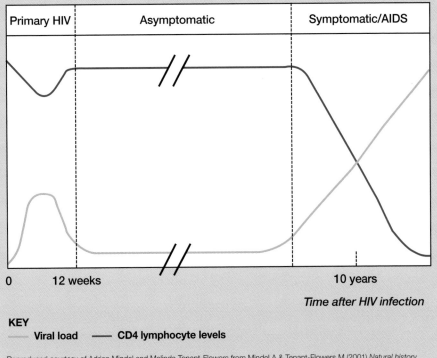

KEY
Viral load —— CD4 lymphocyte levels

Reproduced courtesy of Adrian Mindel and Melinda Tenant-Flowers from Mindel A & Tenant-Flowers M (2001) *Natural history and management of early HIV infection* in Adler MW (ed) *ABC of AIDS*. London: BMJ Publishing Group.

if antiretroviral therapy (ART) is acting effectively. A rising viral load in a patient on ART can indicate a range of problems – for example drug resistance may be developing, or the patient may not be taking their treatment.

The viral load can range from less than 50 copies/ml of plasma (below the level of detection of most currently available assays – often called an 'undetectable' viral load) to over a million copies/ml. The aim of ART is to reduce the viral load to below 50 copies/ml. Numbers of copies per ml can go so high that results are often expressed in a log scale (eg 10^6 copies/ml).

For more on the effects of ART see p56

How the CD4 count and viral load inter-relate

If HIV is replicating out of control but the CD4 count has not yet declined, then the viral load will indicate a problem before the CD4 count. The CD4 count of people who are not on ART and who have a high viral load (for example over 10^4 copies/ml) will drop more quickly than that of those with a lower viral load.

Once the viral load is suppressed, then the CD4 count (and the patient's immunity) has a chance to recover.

There is wide variation in the time it takes to progress from primary infection to symptomatic disease. Figure 5 shows the average.

For more on
types of ART
see p56

Antiretroviral therapy (ART)

ART limits HIV replication. It has had an enormous impact on morbidity and mortality from HIV disease in the UK, as illustrated in figure 1. New drugs and strategies are continually being developed.

The management of HIV has become more complex with the advent of antiretroviral drugs. This section gives a brief overview of the current specialist management of HIV. For aspects of management that may be encountered by the GP, see the guide to managing HIV-related problems on page 75.

Antiretroviral drugs are classified into four groups, according to where and how they act in the replication cycle of the virus. They are:
- nucleoside/nucleotide reverse transcriptase inhibitors (NRTIs)
- non-nucleoside reverse transcriptase inhibitors (NNRTIs)
- protease inhibitors (PIs)
- fusion inhibitors.

Because HIV readily mutates as it replicates, resistance to single anti-HIV drugs develops very readily. This means that currently three or more drugs are used in combinations, and that adherence to drug regimens is essential.

Monitoring of ART is primarily by viral load. Clinicians are also able to access information on the resistance of the strain of HIV in an individual patient and this helps guide drug choice.

After ART has started, the combination of drugs may be changed according to any side effects experienced. These will often be minor but can include more serious conditions such as hyperlipidaemia, diabetes and lipodystrophy (a syndrome characterised by redistribution of body fat).

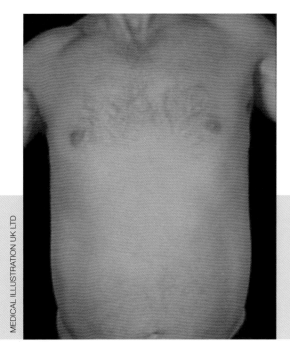

Lipodystrophy.
A syndrome probably caused by
ART and characterised
by redistribution of
body fat.

For more on
lipodystrophy
see p61

HIV prevention in the UK

At a strategic level, efforts to promote sexual health target those in groups associated with a higher risk of HIV. It is sensible, for example, to prioritise interventions supporting safer sex with gay men, or projects working on knowledge of HIV and transmission risks among African communities. However, when faced with an individual patient, those working in primary care can make no assumptions about risk. Each individual's risk needs to be assessed.

For more on assessing risk see p41

Promoting safer sexual practices

Penetrative sex

Condom use significantly reduces the likelihood of sexually transmitted infection (STI) and HIV transmission for both vaginal and anal sex. Condoms should be worn before penetration, and water-based lubricant should be used (oil-based lubricants degrade latex). Recent research has suggested that adequate lubrication may be more important than condom thickness in preventing condom failure. People at risk of acquiring or transmitting HIV should use condoms consistently.

Oral sex

For further information see *Oral sex and transmission of HIV – statement of risk* at www.dh.gov.uk

There is increasing evidence that oral sex, which is common in both heterosexual and homosexual relationships, can allow HIV transmission – especially in the presence of oral disease (ulceration, gingivitis). For some individuals this remains the only risk factor in acquiring HIV infection. The use of (flavoured) condoms for oral sex can reduce the risk. Latex sheets called dental dams are available to cover women's genitalia during oral sex.

Preventing mother-to-child transmission

With appropriate interventions the transmission rate of HIV from mother to baby (vertical transmission) can be reduced from about 20 per cent to under one per cent. Achieving this depends on detecting HIV before or during pregnancy.

The interventions to prevent vertical transmission are:
- antiretroviral therapy in pregnancy
- antiretroviral treatment at delivery plus a short course for the baby
- elective caesarian section (the value of this is now being questioned in women with very low viral loads)
- avoidance of breastfeeding.

All pregnant women should be offered screening for rubella antibody, syphilis, HIV and hepatitis B as an integral part of their antenatal care during their first and all subsequent pregnancies. Antenatal testing for HIV should be recommended.

See Department of Health (2003) *Screening for infectious diseases in pregnancy: standards to support the UK antenatal screening programme.*

> ⚠ **This symbol indicates urgent conditions or highly important information**

Screening blood and treating blood products

All blood donations in the UK are screened for HIV. Since the introduction of screening, there have been only two proven incidents of blood infected with HIV being accepted for transfusion in the UK (still antibody negative because of the window period). All blood products in the UK are heat-treated.

Preventing transmission among injecting drug users

Preventing people from taking up injecting drug use through education and information strategies is one approach.

For those already injecting drugs, there are:

* services supporting people trying to quit, and prescribing safer substitutes such as methadone or buprenorphine
* services supporting safer injecting practices. Needle exchanges are available in some areas. Drug users can exchange used needles and syringes for new replacements on an anonymous basis.

Providing post-exposure prophylaxis (PEP): an emergency

> ⚠

PEP is the emergency use of antiretroviral therapy (ART) to prevent transmission when a person has been at high risk of exposure to HIV. The aim is to give ART within hours of exposure. The exact choice of drug combination requires expert guidance. The medication, usually taken for four weeks, can have significant side effects, and many people are unable to continue working while taking the prophylaxis.

* If exposure to HIV is thought to have occurred through a needle stick injury, urgent advice should be sought.
* If a condom ruptures, exposing to HIV the uninfected sexual partner of someone known to be infected, many HIV treatment centres consider it appropriate to offer PEP. Some will offer it in other circumstances where there has been signficant sexual risk. This is an issue of much debate and is discussed in Department of Health guidance.

See UK Health Departments (2004) *HIV post-exposure prophylaxis: guidance from the UK Chief Medical Officers' Expert Advisory Group on AIDS.*

Immunisation

Most experts agree there is little prospect for an effective vaccine in the near future.

SECTION 2

How to diagnose HIV in primary care

How to diagnose HIV in primary care

People who are unaware that they have HIV are attending primary care. Which symptoms and conditions may be clues to HIV infection? How should HIV testing be approached in primary care?

Opportunities to diagnose HIV in primary care

There are two general circumstances which provide valuable opportunities to diagnose HIV infection in primary care:

- clinical diagnosis when the patient presents with symptoms or medical conditions suggestive of HIV. This is discussed in the first part of this section
- offering an HIV test to an asymptomatic patient because they are or may be at risk of HIV infection. This is included in the second part of this section.

For HIV testing in primary care see p40

Opportunities to diagnose HIV in primary care. Be aware of symptoms and risks for HIV.

CHRIS PRIEST & MARK CLARKE/SCIENCE PHOTO LIBRARY

Talking to patients about HIV

This may be challenging for clinicians – especially if they have to raise the subject with a patient who is not expecting it. Throughout the booklet we suggest verbal strategies that may be used in a variety of clinical situations.

There are three important principles

Be open with the patient about the clinical reasoning behind your questions

- A patient with a skin rash who is suddenly asked 'Can I ask if you are gay?' will wonder what the doctor is up to and, if he is gay, whether it is wise to answer honestly. He may not engage well with the process of giving information. If, however, the doctor first lays out the clinical grounds for asking the question, the patient may be better prepared to give a full history. There are examples of how to do this later in the booklet.

Be non-judgmental

- It is advisable to be direct but sensitive in your questioning. The more accessible and understanding you appear, the more trusting the patient will be, and the more accurate the replies. If patients perceive the clinician to be disapproving or judgmental, then they may be more likely to withhold information that is valuable for their clinical care. They may also not return for future care and follow-up.

Ensure your service is (and is seen to be) confidential

- Some patients have great concerns about confidentiality, in primary care in particular. This may inhibit them from talking openly about highly personal issues. Ensure your practice develops a confidentiality policy and implements it through training and induction, then let your patients know that the policy is in place by displaying a confidentiality statement.

For practice policies and systems see p67

The clinical diagnosis of HIV

There is evidence that a significant proportion of people who present late with HIV infection have been in contact with doctors in preceding years with symptoms which, in retrospect, were clearly related to HIV. Late diagnosis of HIV infection contributes substantially to morbidity and mortality. More advanced disease leaves people vulnerable to overwhelming infection until their CD4 count has risen in response to treatment.

The clinical diagnosis of HIV-related conditions in primary care is not always easy. Many of the problems associated with HIV are commonly seen in people without HIV – for example, seborrhoeic dermatitis, shingles, folliculitis or a glandular fever-like illness. It barely seems feasible to consider HIV – and then to raise it – whenever common conditions such as these present in the surgery. Nevertheless, GPs are familiar with the concept of considering rare but serious conditions when extremely common symptoms present. We make quick assessments to answer questions such as 'Could this febrile child have meningitis?' or 'Could this headache be due to a brain tumour?'. In this section we try to give the GP a realistic and pragmatic approach to improving their chances of detecting HIV infection.

There are two main clinical opportunities for diagnosing symptomatic HIV infection in primary care:
- primary HIV infection (HIV seroconversion illness)
- conditions associated with longstanding HIV infection.

These are dealt with in turn.

Primary HIV infection (HIV seroconversion illness)

Primary HIV infection occurs soon after infection with HIV – usually between two and six weeks. Symptoms develop in over 60 per cent of people at this stage, but they may be mild and non-specific. Even a very HIV-aware GP is likely to miss patients with primary HIV infection.

Diagnosis of primary HIV infection is valuable because:
- the next opportunity for diagnosis may be at a late stage of disease progression, and so the prognosis for the patient is likely to be much worse
- identifying the infection may protect other people from becoming infected by this patient
- the value of antiretrovirals in primary HIV infection is being investigated.

important!

The HIV antibody test is not an appropriate diagnostic test to use if primary HIV infection is suspected, because it may be positive, negative or equivocal (borderline) during this phase of illness. See 'HIV p24 antigen' on page 15.

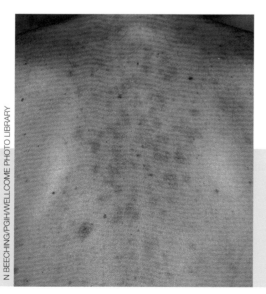

N BEECHING/PGIH/WELLCOME PHOTO LIBRARY

Primary HIV infection.
A blotchy rash on the trunk is sometimes present 2-6 weeks after infection with HIV.

Symptoms and signs of primary HIV infection

The patient may have none, some or all of these:
- fever
- sore throat
- malaise/lethargy
- arthralgia and myalgia
- lymphadenopathy.

If you are thinking of glandular fever – try to remember to consider HIV.

Symptoms and signs that are sometimes also present and are more specific to primary HIV infection include:
- a blotchy rash affecting the trunk
- orogenital or perianal ulceration.

Other features that are less commonly present include:
- headache or meningism
- diarrhoea.

Sometimes the CD4 count drops acutely at this stage of HIV infection, and so acute conditions associated with immunosuppression may also occur, such as:
- oral candidiasis
- shingles
- other conditions associated with immunodeficiency (see pages 27-36).

What to do if you suspect primary HIV infection

Nothing is going to make this an easy consultation. Take a history and, if necessary, conduct an examination to look for further evidence of primary HIV infection. Has the person had a rash? Or sores or ulcers in the mouth or genital area?

If you remain concerned, raise the subject with the patient. 'Illnesses like this are usually caused by viruses, for example the glandular fever or flu virus. Some quite rare viruses can also be a cause, and it is important that I don't miss them if they occur. I have no idea if you are at risk, but HIV is one of these.'

Discuss risks within the last 12 weeks. 'Could I ask you a few questions to see if you could be at risk?'

If you think the patient has primary HIV infection, you should seek urgent advice from a specialist.

For more on risk assessment see p41

useful info

Remember that an HIV antibody test may be negative, even if HIV is the cause (see page 15.)

A man with a flu like illness

Mr I, a 28-year-old, had been registered with the practice two years, but had only attended once before, for smoking cessation advice. He attended his GP saying he had flu and felt dreadful. He said he was exhausted and was now in the eighth day of his illness. He had a sore throat, ached all over and felt feverish.

It was the severity and duration of the symptoms that made the GP consider glandular fever and HIV. First, the GP asked the patient about rashes (he had none) and oral and genital ulceration. The patient said he had mouth ulcers. On examination the GP could see three.

After discussing glandular fever, the GP raised the subject of HIV, and explained that very rarely an illness like this might be caused in the early weeks of HIV infection. The GP took a partner history and established that Mr I lived with his male partner, a relationship of six years. Mr I indicated that he felt that his relationship was mutually monogamous. There was no history of drug use.

The discussion appeared to make the patient anxious, so the GP said: 'On the basis of what you have told me your illness is unlikely to be primary HIV infection.' The GP asked if the patient would be interested in having an HIV test 'in any case' and the patient said he would consider it. The patient returned within a week and explained that he had had unprotected sex five weeks before with a new partner whom he met in a club. He had now discussed the situation fully with his partner at home, and had decided to have a test. Having spoken to an on-call microbiologist, the GP took a sample which was to be tested for HIV antibodies and the HIV p24 antigen. The latter test was positive but the HIV antibody test was negative, confirming primary HIV infection. Mr I was initially distressed and overwhelmed by feelings of guilt. Hospital follow-up was arranged.

Mr I's long-term partner, Mr W, was also registered with the practice. The couple were seen together and it was established that they had had one episode of unprotected sex between the time Mr I had contracted the infection and the time he initially saw the GP. Then they didn't have sex until some time after HIV infection was confirmed. Mr W tested negative both initially and three months later. Six months after this the relationship had survived and the couple were continuing to practise safer sex. Mr I was optimistic and had returned to work. The couple told the GP that they felt that Mr W had been saved from getting HIV because the GP had been 'so on the ball'.

> The HIV p24 antigen test was positive, but the HIV antibody test was negative, confirming primary HIV infection.

> **⚠ This symbol indicates urgent conditions or highly important information**

Clinical conditions associated with longstanding HIV infection

The problems caused by HIV infection are sometimes subtle and insidious, and patients may recover and be well for some time before encountering another problem. Subtle symptoms may mask serious illness, and conditions GPs may have been trained to think were harmless may now indicate HIV disease.

When you encounter any of the conditions given in this section, try to allow the thought of HIV to go through your mind. The stakes are very high for these patients – HIV diagnosis at this presentation may be life-saving. The possibility of immunosuppression is especially important to explore if:

- the patient has had more than one of the conditions listed below in the preceding two or three years; or
- the patient has had unusually severe or difficult to treat forms of the conditions listed below.

Several of the most serious problems listed occur at very low CD4 counts, so they are unlikely to be the first presentation of HIV disease and there are likely to be significant other clinical clues present.

Don't miss urgent or life-threatening conditions
Don't miss PCP

Memorise the conditions that are highlighted in this section using the symbol on the right.

Most serious problems occur at very low CD4 counts (below 100) so other clinical clues to immunosuppression are likely to be present.

Pneumocystis pneumonia (PCP) is an exception to this rule as it tends to occur at higher CD4 counts (below 200). It may be the first HIV-related problem for which the patient seeks advice. The prognosis correlates directly with how early or late the infection is identified and treated: PCP can kill if diagnosed too late.

Guidance on assessment of problems that may be HIV-related

- **Enquire** about weight loss, sweats, diarrhoea
- **Examine** the patient for other signs of immunosuppression (mouth, skin and nodes)
- **Review** the records for evidence of HIV-associated problems in the last three years
- **Discuss** the possibility of HIV with the patient to consider their risk
- **Decide** on priorities: is urgent assessment by a specialist required or can an HIV test be offered?

Mouth, skin and nodes see p32-34

1. Respiratory conditions

Cough, sweats, shortness of breath and weight loss may be caused by several opportunistic infections, including 'ordinary' bacterial infections. *Pneumocystis* pneumonia (PCP) is the most important infection not to miss in the short term. TB is also important. Occasionally, lymphomas or Kaposi's sarcoma may affect the lungs in HIV infected patients.

PCP

This is a life-threatening infection with symptoms which may have an insidious onset progressing over several weeks. Arguably, PCP is the single most dangerous trap for the unwary GP as it may be the first HIV-related clinical problem the patient has. The prognosis correlates directly with how early or late the infection is identified and treated: PCP can kill if diagnosed late.

Symptoms

- a persistent dry cough of a few weeks duration
- increasing shortness of breath or decreasing exercise tolerance: 'I first noticed it when I ran for a bus, but now I feel short of breath just sitting'
- difficulty in taking a full breath (this reflects loss of elasticity of the lung tissue)
- fever (in most but not all)

Assessment

The chest may be clear on auscultation – especially in early stages. Fine crackles may be heard. Chest X-rays may reveal little and can lead to delay. The GP may be thinking of asthma, an atypical chest infection or anxiety. If PCP is a possibility, look for evidence of HIV: see the guidance for assessment on page 27 and also boxed information on page 36.

If PCP is a possibility, look for evidence of HIV.

Management/referral

Refer patients urgently if you are concerned they may have PCP, which can only be diagnosed by hospital-based tests such as sputum cytology (and often bronchoscopy). An HIV antibody test may cause inappropriate delay.

This condition is also important to detect in any patients known to have HIV, and who have CD4 counts of less than 200, even if they are on medication to prevent this.

TB and atypical mycobacterial disease

TB is an important and common presenting problem in HIV-infected patients in the UK. It can occur at CD4 counts above 200. Atypical mycobacterial disease *(mycobacterium avium intracellulare)* is a less common complication, associated with late stage HIV infection.

Symptoms

Patients may have a cough, fever, sweats, shortness of breath, weight loss or haemoptysis. They may have associated large, asymmetrical nodes.

Mycobacterium avium intracellulare may present with systemic symptoms and chest symptoms may or may not be present. Abnormal liver function, or anaemia may be found.

Assessment

For guidance on assessment see box on p27

Your usual assessment for TB (eg CXR) and look for evidence of HIV: see guidance on assessment on page 27 and boxed information on page 36. *Mycobacterium avium intracellulare* is very unlikely in a patient without several clinical pointers to HIV disease, because it occurs at very low CD4 counts.

Management/referral

For RCP guidelines on HIV testing, see Rogstad et al (2004) HIV testing for patients attending general medical services:concise guidelines. *Clin Med* **4**:136-9.

Urgent outpatient or inpatient referral will be required, although an HIV test could also be arranged and may save time if the patient is not too unwell. National guidelines on HIV testing from the Royal College of Physicians (RCP) recommend that all patients with indicator diseases (including TB) or symptoms be offered HIV testing.

'Ordinary' chest infections

Chest infections which respond to the antibiotics usually employed in community settings are commoner in immunosuppressed patients.

Assessment

Look for evidence of HIV: see guidance on assessment on page 27.

Management/referral

As usual for chest infections, but offer an HIV test if appropriate.

2. Conditions causing neurological and visual symptoms

A great variety of intracranial or peripheral neurological problems may occur in relation to HIV infection. Symptoms and signs include:

- headache, neck stiffness or photophobia
- focal neurological signs suggesting intracranial space occupying lesion
- peripheral neuropathy (especially sensory change or loss)
- confusion, memory loss, or disinhibition
- fits.

Cryptococcal meningitis

This may present with headaches without the classical symptoms or signs of meningism.

Assessment

Apart from a neurological assessment and general examination, look for evidence of HIV. See guidance on assessment on page 27.

Management/referral

The patient will need to be referred urgently. An HIV test may not be appropriate if the patient is very unwell.

Cytomegalovirus (CMV) infection of the retina

CMV infection of the retina causes blindness and is treatable only if caught early. It is also important to detect in those patients known to have HIV, and who have CD4 counts of less than 100.
The patient may have:

- floaters
- reduced vision
- scotomas.

Pain is not a feature.

For CD4 counts see p15

Assessment

For guidance on assessment see box on p27

Changes may be visible on fundoscopy, but the absence of changes should not alter management. Look for evidence of HIV: see guidance on assessment on page 27. CMV retinitis is very unlikely in a patient without several clinical pointers to HIV disease, because it occurs at very low CD4 counts.

Management/referral

The patient will need to be referred urgently to ophthalmology.

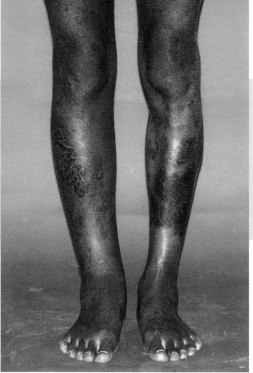

Kaposi's sarcoma.
This tumour is associated with immunosuppression and has a variety of appearances on the skin.

3. Tumours associated with HIV

Lymphoma
Lymphoma may cause lymphadenopathy, fevers, night sweats and abdominal masses. It may be cerebral (see neurological problems, page 30).

Assessment
Look for evidence of HIV. See guidance on assessment on page 27.

Management/referral
As for any suspected cancer. It may be appropriate to arrange an HIV test.

Cervical carcinoma
Cervical cancer may cause vaginal bleeding or discharge.
Cytological abnormalities may also be a marker for underlying HIV infection.

Assessment and management/referral
As normal for suspected cervical cancer. Offer an HIV test if appropriate.

Kaposi's sarcoma (KS)
These tumours may occur in a variety of places. They most commonly appear as dark purple or brown intradermal lumps that sometimes look like bruises (but feel harder). KS may also be found in the mouth. Infiltration of the lungs or gut is rare but can be very serious, the latter causing GI bleeding. KS may cause weight loss.

Assessment and management/referral
Refer to HIV specialist. May require urgent medical admission if lung or gut involvement.

4. Constitutional symptoms associated with HIV

Constitutional symptoms may be caused by HIV itself, or by a related opportunistic infection (such as TB) or tumour (such as a lymphoma). Symptoms include:

- fever
- weight loss
- sweats
- lymphadenopathy (HIV is particularly likely if this persists in excess of three months, in two or more extra-inguinal sites and in the absence of any other cause).

For guidance on assessment see box on p27

Assessment

Look for evidence of HIV.

Management/referral

Urgent outpatient or inpatient assessment is sometimes appropriate. Alternatively arrange an HIV test.

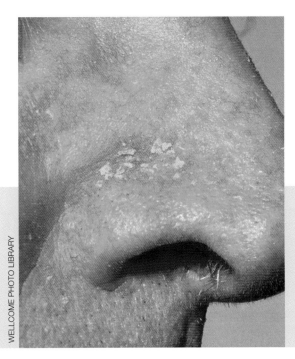

WELLCOME PHOTO LIBRARY

Seborrhoeic dermatitis.
This common condition may give a clue to immunosuppression, especially if severe or difficult to treat.

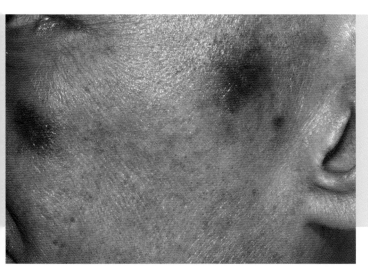

Kaposi's sarcoma.
This tumour may also
rarely affect the gut
or lungs.

5. Skin conditions

Look out for common skin conditions that are particularly severe or hard to treat. Review the records for other evidence of HIV infection. Examples include:

- **fungal infections**, such as *tinea cruris*, *tinea pedis*, *pityriasis versicolor*
- **viral infections**, such as shingles (especially if more than one dermatome is affected), *molluscum contagiosum*, warts and herpes simplex
- **bacterial infections**, such as impetigo, folliculitis
- **Kaposi's sarcoma** (see description on page 31 and photographs on pages 31 and 33)
- **other skin conditions**, such as seborrhoeic dermatitis (see photo opposite) and psoriasis.

Assessment

Look for evidence of HIV. See guidance on assessment on page 27, and also boxed information on page 36.

Management/referral

As usual, and arrange an HIV test if appropriate.

6. Conditions affecting the mouth

Immunosuppression can lead to a number of conditions affecting the mouth, and examination of the mouth is key in assessment, as some of the conditions may be asymptomatic. Examples include:

- **oral candidiasis** (thrush): not just a coated tongue, but thick white plaques on the buccal mucosa that can be scraped off with a tongue depressor. Swabs are of little diagnostic value because of high carriage rates.
- **aphthous ulceration**
- **oral hairy leukoplakia**: causing whitish corrugations, typically on the side of the tongue. They cannot be scraped off. It is usually asymptomatic, but is pathognomonic of immunosupression. It is useful to look for this if you suspect a patient may have HIV disease
- **Kaposi's sarcoma**: purple tumour, characteristically on the palate (see page 35)
- gingivitis
- dental abscesses.

> **important!**
>
> Florid oral thrush should always lead to a consideration of whether the patient could be immunosuppressed

Assessment

Look for evidence of HIV: see guidance on assessment on page 27, and also boxed information on page 36.

Management/referral

As usual and arrange an HIV test if appropriate.

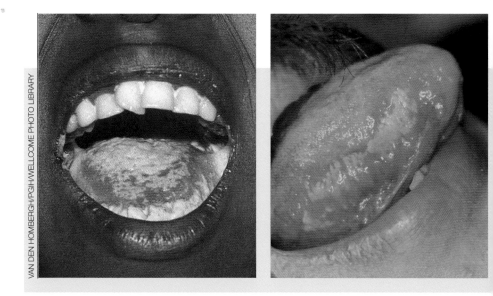

VAN DEN HOMBERGH/PGIH/WELLCOME PHOTO LIBRARY

7. Conditions affecting the upper and lower GI tract

Significant conditions include:

- **oesophageal candidiasis**: the patient presents with dysphagia suggestive of an oesophageal problem, but is highly likely to have concurrent oral thrush
- **diarrhoea** – persistent mild, or severe acute. There may be virtually any – or commonly no – causative organism found.

For guidance on assessment see box on p27

Assessment

Look for evidence of HIV.

Management/referral

As usual and arrange an HIV test if appropriate.

8. Genital problems

See also cervical cancer on p31

Sexually transmitted infections (STIs) such as genital herpes or genital warts may be more severe in the immunosuppressed patient. In addition, severe or difficult to treat genital candida may itself be a clue to immunosuppression. The diagnosis of any STI should lead to a consideration of the possibility of other STIs, including HIV.

Assessment

Look for evidence of HIV: see guidance on assessment on page 27, and also boxed information on page 36.

Management/referral

As usual and arrange an HIV test if appropriate.

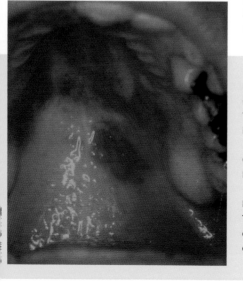

From left to right:

Oral candida.
This condition is an important indicator of immunosuppression.

Oral hairy leukoplakia.
Pathognomonic of immunosuppression.

Palatal Kaposi's sarcoma.
This tumour gives another reason for careful examination of the mouth when looking for evidence of HIV.

9. Haematological problems

Changes found on routine full blood counts may give a clue to immunosuppression. They may be severe enough to require urgent action, but are often more subtle, with few symptoms.
Examples include:

- neutropenia
- anaemia
- thrombocytopaenia.

Assessment

Look for evidence of HIV. See guidance on assessment on page 27 and box below.

For guidance on assessment see box on p27

Management/referral

As usual and arrange an HIV test if appropriate.

What to do if you suspect HIV infection may underlie the presenting problem

If the problem is clinically minor (seborrhoeic dermatitis in a patient who had multidermatomal shingles two months ago), it may be reasonable to arrange an early review of the patient in order to give yourself time to collect your thoughts. But don't risk losing patients to follow-up. Remember that resolution of the presenting problem does not mean that HIV has been ruled out.

- **Enquire** about weight loss, sweats, diarrhoea
- **Examine** the patient for other signs of immunosuppression (mouth, skin and nodes, see pages 32-34)
- **Review** the records for evidence of HIV-associated problems in the last three years (see list, pages 28-36)
- **Discuss** the possibility of HIV with the patient to consider their risk.

For many GPs – quite understandably – raising the subject with the patient is the difficult bit. Something along the lines of the following formulae might work: 'The problems that you have had recently are quite common, and usually minor. However, very occasionally they can give a clue that your immune system is not working as well as it should.' 'I don't know if you are at risk of HIV, but this is one condition that can affect the immune system. Could I ask you some questions to see if you could be at risk?' .

For more details on risk assessment, see p41

- **Decide on priorities:** is urgent assessment by a specialist required or can an HIV test be offered?

If the clinical picture is strongly suggestive of HIV, an apparent absence of risk of infection should not deter the GP from offering the patient a test 'From what you tell me you are quite unlikely to have HIV. Do you think it would be wise to do a test anyway so that we can be sure?'

---

case history

Late diagnosis of HIV and tuberculosis

Miss J is a 26-year-old woman who came to the UK from Sierra Leone two years ago. She saw her GP with a six-week history of fevers, intermittent cough and cervical lymphadenopathy. Nine months previously she had attended her GP with fatigue and was found to have mild anaemia. Now she was prescribed Penicillin V, which alleviated her symptoms for a few days. A week later she presented again with rigors, night sweats and weight loss. She was admitted to hospital for investigation of a 'pyrexia of unknown origin' with malaria at the top of the differential diagnosis.

She was found to have non-tender 'rubbery' lymphadenopathy in her axilliary, inguinal, supraclavicular and cervical areas. On admission she also had a fever of 39.4°C and a tachycardia. She was hypotensive, had

She had been complaining of non-specific fatigue/malaise for at least eight or nine months, for which the full blood count had been the only investigation.

2-3cms hepatomegaly and otherwise no focal signs in her chest, abdomen or CNS.

She was treated with multiple antibiotics but did not improve. Following discussion with a member of the HIV team she reluctantly agreed to a test for HIV antibodies, which was positive. She was eventually diagnosed with tuberculosis following sputum culture.

The history that emerged when she felt better was that she had been feeling 'ill' for at least six to eight weeks, and had had intermittent fevers (and some night sweats) for three months. She had been complaining of non-specific fatigue/malaise for at least eight or nine months, for which the full blood count had been the only investigation. She might not have agreed to an HIV test at this time, but an earlier diagnosis might have enabled her to avoid hospitalisation.

case history

A newly registered African woman

Miss H is a 34-year-old Zimbabwean who had just registered with her GP. Her new patient check noted that her child had died in Zimbabwe before she came to this country three years ago. When her records came they showed she had had a previous abnormal smear (CIN 1).

Miss H attended the surgery because of recurrent genital itching. She described her current health as good. On examination she was found to have genital herpes and *molluscum contagiosum*. The GP also found cervical lymphadenopathy. She had no other rashes and no oral conditions suggestive of

HIV. On further questioning her GP ascertained she had no history of previous sexually transmitted infections and had never been tested for HIV. The GP suggested that an HIV test was done, and the patient agreed. The result was positive, information which Miss H took surprisingly well.

Miss H was referred to the HIV clinic and soon after commenced on ART. Currently, she is quite well and continues to work. On several occasions since her diagnosis she has thanked her GP for suggesting the HIV test. She had felt she was not at risk and is glad that she had the test before she became seriously unwell.

case history

A 'low-risk' man

Mr R is a 33-year-old university lecturer of UK origin who first presented to the practice nurse during a new patient medical following a house move. He lived with his girlfriend of eight years. At registration he complained of a rash on his face. This was red, dry and flaky and affected his forehead and his naso-labial folds. He was given a topical hydrocortisone/antifungal cream.

Twelve months later he returned to the practice and saw a locum GP following three days of non-specific abdominal pain and fever. He returned again to the practice after 10 days with a dry cough, fatigue and lethargy. He was given a broad-spectrum antibiotic but 14 days later was worse, and had developed a generalised maculo-papular rash. The facial rash had returned, since he had run out of cream. He had lost 4kg of weight.

Frustrated at being off work for so long, he requested a referral to the local hospital where he was seen by a consultant physician three weeks later. Tests carried out by the GP in advance revealed a slight thrombocytopaenia, mild elevation of his liver transaminases and a raised ESR. A chest X-ray was reported as normal. Mr R was asked if he had ever injected drugs and stated that he had not

done so. Serology for hepatitis B was negative. Physical examination by the hospital consultant revealed no abnormalities and an ultrasound of his liver was arranged.

Another three weeks passed, with no scan appointment arriving. Mr R reported a worsening of his cough and extreme fatigue. He had marked dyspnoea on exertion. Two days later his girlfriend took him to casualty. By this time his dyspnoea had worsened, his weight loss continued and he had a dry cough. He was found to be tachypnoeic and hypoxic. His CXR showed patchy shadowing. The medical team felt he probably had *pneumocystis* pneumonia (PCP). This was later confirmed on bronchoscopy. Mr R tested positive for HIV antibodies and his CD4 count was only 10. Following the successful treatment of his PCP and initiation of antiretroviral therapy, he returned to work and remains well.

With no apparent risk factors to suggest a significant probability of HIV infection, and with such an insidious onset, the diagnosis eluded many practitioners until Mr R was quite seriously ill. It is probable that he acquired HIV through a sexual contact many years previously when he was travelling in Thailand and the Far East in his student years.

> With no apparent risk factors to suggest a significant probability of HIV infection, and with such an insidious onset, the diagnosis eluded many practitioners until Mr R was quite seriously ill.

case history

A delayed diagnosis

Mr G is a 49-year-old divorced architect. He attended his GP some months ago with diarrhoea and weight loss. Stool culture/microscopy revealed no apparent pathogen and there was little response to anti-diarrhoeal medication. He was referred to the local hospital where he was seen and placed on the waiting list for both upper GI endoscopy and a flexible sigmoidoscopy. This was performed four months after the original referral letter, his symptoms having continued and his overall weight loss being some 10 per cent of his original weight.

After the procedure he had to stay in hospital for two nights as he appeared to have developed an aspiration pneumonia. Broad-spectrum antibiotic treatment did very little and he was re-admitted four days later. Bronchoscopy confirmed a diagnosis of PCP, for which he was admitted and treated without further complication.

The only recorded social history was that he was divorced and smoked 20 cigarettes daily. He was not embarrassed to tell the doctors that he had sex with other men, but nobody had ever asked him. He was not surprised by the subsequent HIV diagnosis. His CD4 count was 49 and he has done well since starting combination antiretroviral therapy.

He was not embarrassed to tell the doctors that he had sex with other men, but nobody had ever asked him.

HIV testing in primary care

Reducing the amount of undiagnosed HIV in the UK is a priority. Individuals who know they are infected with HIV have significant advantages over those who are infected but unaware of this. They will:

- benefit from the effectiveness of current treatments resulting in a radically improved prognosis
- have information which may enable them to reduce further transmission of the virus
- have the opportunity to reflect and plan ahead.

1. The practicalities
What is the HIV test?

It is a test for antibodies to HIV. It is important to remember that the test may not become positive until three months after the person has become infected (the window period).

> For an account of the HIV antibody test see p15

For an account of the HIV antibody test see p15

useful info

Recent joint guidelines provide more detailed advice for doctors (Association of British Insurers & British Medical Association (2002) *Medical information and insurance: joint guidelines from the British Medical Association and the Association of British Insurers*). Insurers should only ask the applicant whether they have tested positive for HIV. See also updated guidance on confidentiality from the GMC, *Confidentiality: protecting and providing information* (2004) at www.gmc-uk.org. GPs should be guided by clinical need above all other considerations.

HIV testing and insurance reports

GPs should not allow insurance concerns to compromise patient care: if an HIV test is appropriate, it should be offered. In the past there has been a reluctance to use HIV tests as a diagnostic tool in primary care. This may be due, in part, to concerns about the possibility that a doctor or patient may have to declare HIV testing (regardless of result) on a GP insurance report form. However, as long ago as 1994 the Association of British Insurers stated that a previous negative HIV test should not affect the application.

Laboratory support

The lab will need a clotted sample. Some smaller hospital laboratories only run HIV antibody tests on certain days. Phone the lab to check:

- when HIV tests are processed
- when the results will be available
- what their procedure will be if they find an apparent positive.

Links with specialist HIV treatment centre(s)

The best time to find out about local HIV treatment centres, and establish links with them, is before you have a patient who tests positive. In this way, clear referral pathways can be in place, including details of who to contact if a patient needs to be seen urgently by a specialist.

Computer and paper systems to support HIV testing

See page 68 for discussion of systems and record keeping.

2. When should an HIV antibody test be offered?

There are a number of circumstances in which it is appropriate to conduct an HIV test:

- the patient may request an HIV test
- the patient may have an identified risk
- the patient may have symptoms or signs of HIV disease
- the patient may be in a group offered screening tests for HIV.

The patient who requests an HIV test

Patients requesting an HIV test will have a reason – you may choose to be reassuring but avoid discouraging patients from testing and take care before declining to test.

Be flexible: some people with HIV may have no apparent risk. Patients may or may not be prepared to discuss their risks with you. You do not always need to know what risk there was, as long as the patient understands the significance of the three-month window period and what constitutes risk. If doubts remain, arrange a second test in three months.

The patient may have an identified risk

Because HIV infection can be asymptomatic for so long, the only hope of improving primary care detection rates in this group is if clinicians are willing and able to discuss risk of HIV and offer tests as appropriate. Risk of HIV can be identified through taking a drug and sexual history for the purposes of health promotion.

The following people should be offered a test if they have never been tested, or if they have had further risk since their last test. Those who:

- have a current or former sexual partner who is infected with HIV, or from an area with a high prevalence of HIV or who was an injecting drug user
- have had anal or oral sex between men (though the latter is much lower risk)
- are from an area with a high prevalence of HIV (although risk should be discussed without pre-judgment as many people in this group may be at no risk)
- have had multiple sexual partners
- have a history of sexually transmitted infection
- have a history of injecting drug use
- have been raped (although in an acute situation this is best managed by specialist services if the patient will attend)
- have had blood transfusions, transplants or other risk prone procedures in countries without rigorous procedures for HIV screening in these circumstances
- may have had an occupational exposure.

Careful condom use may well have offered significant protection – this should be acknowledged, even if testing still goes ahead. Be ready to test

Raising the subject of an HIV test

Communication strategies

- Raise the subject of HIV before a sexual history has been taken – perhaps in a contraception or smear consultation. 'HIV is much more common in people from Africa. Do you know people who have been affected? As it is a serious, but treatable condition, could we discuss whether you might have been at risk?'
- Raise the subject of sexual health in a new patient check. 'We find that quite a lot of young men are at risk of having sexual health problems. Could I ask you a few questions to see if you are at risk?'
- Raise the subject of HIV once a sexual history has been taken. 'Because two of your partners in the last year have been male, like you, it is possible that you are at higher risk of HIV. Have you ever considered having an HIV test?'
- Raise the subject of HIV when a history of injecting drug use has been identified. 'Current advice is that everyone who has injected drugs in the past should be offered a test for HIV, because this condition responds so well to treatment. Have you ever considered having a test?'
- Remember to emphasise the benefits of earlier HIV diagnosis.

For clinical diagnosis see box on p27

anyone who requests an HIV test after their history has been taken, even if they have not indicated a specific risk to you.

The patient may have symptoms or signs suggestive of HIV disease

See pages 23-36 for clinical diagnosis and pages 23 and 36 for communication strategies in this context.

Preventing mother to child transmission see p19

The patient may be in a group offered screening tests for HIV

Screening will sometimes be offered in a specialist setting, and sometimes in primary care. For example:

- **women in antenatal care**, in order to prevent mother to child transmission
- **those found to have conditions which may be associated with HIV** (such as TB, lymphoma, hepatitis B or C, syphilis or other STIs).

It is important that the value of the HIV test is explained to the patient.

important!

Make sure all pregnant women are offered and recommended an HIV test. Interventions can reduce the risk of mother to child transmission from 20% to 1%.

3. The pre-test discussion

Given here is a breakdown of the items that might be covered in a pre-test discussion. Not all areas will need to be covered with all patients. The time a discussion takes is extremely variable. In a well-informed, reasonably low risk person it may take just a few minutes.

See HIV testing aide-memoire on p72

A checklist is given on page 72 which can be used as an aide-memoire by the GP or practice nurse conducting an HIV test.

i) Check the patient's understanding of HIV

Assess their understanding of different transmission routes. They need to be aware of the difference between HIV and AIDS and should be clear about the medical advantage of knowing their HIV status.

Some patients believe that if they have had any blood tests in the past, they will automatically have been tested for HIV.

The patient should understand the significance of the three-month window period and that a repeat test may be needed.

ii) Discuss risk to date

Knowing the nature of the risk enables the clinician to tailor advice on risk reduction, and knowing the timing of risk(s) is important because of the window period (see page 15). If doubt about the window period remains, simply arrange a second test in three months.

See more on the timing of risks on p15

If the patient does not wish to discuss their risk, but wishes to go ahead with a test, they should be able to do so as long as the benefits of discussing risk have been mentioned.

See page 41 for risks that may be discussed. If the patient is unwilling to go into detail, it may be best simply to address the issues on the HIV aide-memoire (page 72) in order to maintain the doctor-patient relationship.

iii) Discuss future risk and risk reduction

This may be the first opportunity that a patient has had to discuss how to keep themselves safe. It may be best to discuss safer sexual practices and safer injecting practices before the test, rather than just when the result is given, not least because risks may be taken before the patient is next seen. If a repeat test is to be arranged, emphasise that HIV transmitted by any risks between now and the next test will not show up in that result.

iv) Discuss the implications of a positive test

How is the patient likely to react if the result is positive? What would their main concerns be if they tested positive? What will be the reactions of those they might tell? What might be the implications for their partner? For their work?

v) Explain confidentiality

Explain that a positive test result will need to be recorded in their medical records so that their healthcare remains safe and appropriate. It will also have to be disclosed to insurance companies if requested (negative tests do not have to be disclosed).

vi) Discuss how they will cope with the wait

- Ask the patient to consider who knows they are having a test, and who it is safe to tell.
- Ask the patient not to drink alcohol or take drugs on the day of the result.
- Consider whether there is any written information that should be given to the patient.

vii) Consider if the test is best conducted in primary care

In people with multiple problems (those with psychological or emotional problems, those with additional counselling needs, or those who may react badly to a positive result) a referral to GUM services for testing may be appropriate. However, this should be balanced against the benefits of having a test conducted in more familiar surroundings and by a clinician known to the patient.

viii) Consider whether other tests are appropriate

It may be appropriate to request other tests at the same time as HIV. For example:

- if the risk is considered to be due to needle sharing, talk to the patient about testing for hepatitis B and C
- if the risk is unprotected sexual intercourse – particularly if the risk appears high – then you may wish to discuss tests for other STIs such as chlamydia, syphilis or hepatitis B.

There is a growing trend for specialist clinics to offer routinely tests for hepatitis B and C, and syphilis, alongside HIV. If your patient proves to be infected with HIV they may arrange these tests.

Consider the need for immunisation against hepatitis B.

xi) Consider whether repeat tests are required

Ensure the patient understands fully if they are going to need a repeat test (to cover the window period) before current HIV infection can be ruled out. Emphasise that HIV acquired by any risks between now and the next test will not show up in the next result.

x) Check whether the patient has given clear consent to HIV (or other) tests

Informed consent must be obtained before any test. You can ask: 'Shall we go ahead with the HIV test?'

xi) Check whether you have their contact details
Record contact details, and check their preferred method of contact and any possible problems with leaving messages or talking. You will be glad of this if the patient fails to attend for a result that turned out to be positive.

xii) Arrange an appointment for the result to be given
Try to ensure that you are not going to give a result at a bad time – for example, a Friday evening surgery. A good rule is to arrange to give the result face to face. If you arrange to give the result by phone, and then later ask the patient to come to the surgery instead, this can cause severe anxiety. If, however, you have arranged to meet face to face but the result is negative, you can always ring them.

xiii) Check if the patient has a supply of appropriate condoms and lubricant

4. Giving the result
If the result is negative, you will need to consider whether the patient needs a further test because of the window period. When giving a negative result, don't forget to reinforce advice about minimising risk, if appropriate.
If the result is positive, there are many things you need to consider before the patient attends.

Preparing to give a positive result
You will have time to collect your thoughts and seek advice, because the lab is likely to phone the result through and ask for a repeat sample. Remember:
- you already have skills in discussing very difficult things
- the patient chose you to do their test, so they chose you to give them the result.

Review the consultation when you took the test:
- what were the patient's main concerns should the test be positive?
- who knew they were being tested?
- where do they get support?
- is there a partner whose needs you should discuss with the patient? (Formal partner notification should be addressed by the HIV clinic.)

Consider referral arrangements:
- the patient will need to be referred to a specialist HIV clinic, so an appointment can be made in advance.
- have available some relevant literature and phone numbers of support organisations.
- see also 'The newly diagnosed person' page 50.

See 'the newly diagnosed person' on p50

When the patient attends

Give the result soon after the patient is in the room and has sat down. Delaying disclosure can heighten anxiety. This also gives you more time to attend to and deal with the patient's reactions. Some patients are expecting a positive result and may be quite calm. Indeed, some may have already come to terms with being positive. But remember a calm exterior can also mask a sense of shock.

You should emphasise the positive aspects; patients are better off knowing that they have HIV.

In the case of a positive result, listen carefully and make the discussion as focused and tailored to the individual as possible. Touch on the issues raised when the test was taken. For example: 'You said last week that if the result was positive your main concern would be… Perhaps we should think about that now.'

You should emphasise the positive aspects; patients are better off knowing that they have HIV.

When the consultation is coming to an end:
- give the patient the details of any appointment that you have arranged
- remember that risk reduction advice to protect partners will need to be addressed, but this may be hard for the patient to take in at this consultation
- consider when you are planning to see them next.

case history

An opportunity to test for HIV

Mr P, aged 26, attended the practice nurse for a new patient check. He was an accountant, and generally fit and well with no significant past medical history. The practice encouraged sexual health promotion, and the nurse raised the subject once other aspects of the check were complete.

She asked him if it was okay if she asked questions to see if he could be at risk of any sexual health problems. He agreed, but seemed to become a bit guarded. The nurse took a partner history according to her routine, avoiding assumptions. The patient opened up and relaxed, and shortly explained that he wasn't living alone as he had told her, but was gay and living with his partner of three years. He felt this relationship was mutually monogamous, but he had had several partners prior to this. She asked about condom use and established that he had had significant risk of exposure to HIV through several 'casual' sexual contacts in years gone by. Mr P explained that he had always meant to have a test for HIV, but never got round to it. He had also discussed it with his partner in the past, but more recently the subject had been forgotten.

After discussion it was agreed that Mr P would suggest to his partner that he also registered 'as it seems a really nice practice'. The nurse agreed she would be happy to arrange an HIV test for both of them. In due course, both attended. The HIV tests were negative. The couple were very grateful to the nurse for having dealt with an issue that had been a suppressed but niggling worry.

> The couple were very grateful to the nurse for having dealt with an issue that had been a suppressed but niggling worry.

Summary: how to improve HIV detection in your practice

Familiarise GPs and practice nurses in the team with:

- the more HIV-specific aspects of primary HIV infection, and be ready to ask about them in patients with a 'glandular fever-like' illness (pages 24-26)
- those urgent conditions that may present in patients whose HIV infection remains undiagnosed, most importantly PCP (pages 27-28)
- those conditions that are associated with HIV infection (pages 27-36), especially if patients have had
  - more than one in the last two to three years, or
  - an unusually difficult to treat or severe form of these conditions
- risk factors for HIV which should prompt an offer of an HIV test (see page 41).

Plan and practise strategies for discussing HIV with patients in different clinical circumstances.

Take steps to incorporate HIV testing into the health promotion work of the practice nurse team.

SECTION 3

Clinical care for the patient with HIV

IN THIS SECTION

Clinical care for the patient with HIV

HIV is increasingly managed as a chronic disease, with many more patients surviving for longer periods. This is shifting the emphasis of care towards partnership between specialist centres and primary care.

Looking after specific groups of people with HIV

1. The newly diagnosed person

Unfortunately, HIV infection is still a stigmatised condition and thus telling friends, family or colleagues is never easy for patients. Some will not be prepared to absorb fully the news of a positive test result. Despite careful pre-test discussion, some may need considerable support over time.

A significant number of women newly diagnosed with HIV have been identified through antenatal screening. Such a woman may be facing a truly challenging range of issues: a newly diagnosed and serious medical condition; pregnancy and whether to continue; the possibility that existing children are infected and the possibility that her partner is infected – all at the same time.

2. The patient who informs you they have HIV

A patient – whether newly registered or not – may inform their GP or practice nurse that they have HIV. They may be quite anxious about divulging this information and may require reassurance that it was helpful to do so. Communication with the specialist clinic (assuming one is involved) should be established as soon as possible. Very occasionally, a patient may be making up their positive HIV status. Whilst it is not ever appropriate to signal disbelief when a patient discloses that they have HIV, a plan should be put in place for confirmation in due course.

3. Gay men

There may be organisations offering support to gay men with HIV infection in your area – your patient may (or may not) wish to be put in touch.

If the patient has a long-term partner, the practice can play a key supporting role – especially if the partner is acting as carer. The partner may be registered with the practice as well, in which case their needs as a carer may be easier to address. Gay partnerships are not legally recognised with respect to inheritance. The patient with deteriorating

For more information on the need to write a will see p64

immunity may need to consider this and contact a solicitor to write a will (see 'The dying patient', page 63).

4. African people

There may be organisations offering support to people with HIV of African origin in your area – your patient may (or may not) wish to be put in touch with them.

Some of these patients are asylum seekers or refugees who may have lost family members to violence and have fled their country. HIV may, for some, be the least of their immediate problems. Some asylum seekers may ultimately be returned to countries where HIV treatment is unavailable to them.

Diagnosis in an adult may immediately lead to concerns about their children, who may well have been born in a country not intervening to prevent vertical transmission.

There may be language difficulties, and consultations with an interpreter may need to be arranged. Finding interpreters may lead to serious concerns about confidentiality for patients living within their community.

5. Injecting drug users

There may be organisations in your area that offer specialist counselling or support to drug users. Some organisations offer specific support for those who are infected with HIV.

Do not assume that all injecting drug users are fully aware of the risks of sharing equipment or using non-sterile needles. It does no harm to repeat and reinforce the message.

Low self-esteem, being in prison, previous abuse and other psycho-emotional problems may be underlying issues that affect this group.

Health promotion, screening and immunisation for patients with HIV

1. Sexual health advice for patients with HIV

Healthcare workers need to be able to discuss sexual practices with patients with HIV. Many people find it difficult to maintain safer sexual practices all the time. Practitioners should aim to be supportive and avoid criticism. It is clearly beneficial if GPs can provide condoms and lubricant.

Sometimes the person with HIV faces difficulties related to disclosure, and further support from an expert counsellor or health adviser can be offered if appropriate. Continued unprotected sex clearly presents a risk of HIV transmission.

Those who are having unprotected sex with partner(s) who are also infected with HIV are still at potential risk of acquiring a drug-resistant strain of HIV or other STIs, so condom use is recommended even in couples where both have HIV. Regular sexual health checks may be important.

2. Cervical screening

Women with HIV (especially if they have a low CD4 count) are more at risk from human papilloma virus-related disease, including cervical cancer and warts. All women with HIV infection should have annual smears with more frequent follow-up and colposcopy if abnormalities are found.

3. Immunisation

The practice can and should play a key role in immunising patients who have HIV. Current advice should always be based on the most recent edition of 'The Green Book' (Department of Health (1996) *Immunisation Against Infectious Disease*), unless practitioners are informed otherwise.

In general, live vaccines should be avoided. Individuals with HIV infection should not normally receive BCG, yellow fever, or oral typhoid. Live oral polio (Sabin) immunisation has now been withdrawn. All inactivated immunisations such as pertussis, diphtheria, tetanus, inactivated polio (Salk), typhoid, and meningitis C are safe.

Check for updates and replacement chapters to The Green Book: www.dh.gov.uk, go to 'immunisation against infectious disease'

Adults with HIV should be offered:
- influenza immunisation each year
- hepatitis B testing and immunisation as appropriate
- hepatitis A immunisation for men who have sex with men.

In addition, they may be offered:
- pneumococcal immunisation.

Specialist advice should be sought from the paediatric team about immunisation of children infected with HIV, and children of parents with HIV.

If a baby is born to a mother with HIV, transmitted infection will usually have been identified by eight weeks. Inactivated polio is now given to all babies as standard. This is safe whether or not a baby is infected with HIV and whether or not family members are immunocompromised.

4. Advice and immunisation for international travel

Hepatitis A and B vaccination should be offered as appropriate.
Malaria prophylaxis is used, but interactions can occur. The antiretroviral, ritonavir, for example, can interact with several antimalarials. Check on www.hiv-druginteractions.org

If a yellow fever certificate is required, then a letter of exemption from a medical practitioner will normally allow entry. The reason for the exemption need not be specified.

For patients with HIV travelling to areas where medical support may be difficult to obtain, GPs might supply a couple of courses of ciprofloxacin for travellers' diarrhoea, together with advice on hygiene and food preparation.

Advice on safer sex and the avoidance of sexually

Check for drug interactions on:
www.hiv-druginteractions.org
transmitted infections may need to be reinforced.

Patients may also be offered a concise medical summary, including prescribed medication, in case of illness abroad.

5. Cardiovascular disease prevention

It is possible that people with HIV are at higher risk from cardiovascular disease. In addition, dyslipidaemias and diabetes are associated with anti-HIV therapy (see 'ART side effects' page 58), although their impact on the cardiovascular system is unclear. Effort should therefore be put into promoting healthy diets, exercise, alcohol control, blood pressure checks and smoking cessation. Bupropion should only be prescribed after obtaining expert advice if people are taking PIs or NNRTIs, because of potential interactions.

See side-effects of ART p58-62

Reproductive health and fertility

1. Contraception

Being HIV positive in itself rarely affects contraceptive prescribing. The woman's choice should be central. Condoms are always recommended, but their relatively high failure rates should be considered before using them alone.

For women on ART: the IUD, IUS or depot medroxyprogesterone acetate injections (at the usual intervals) may be used; the progestogen only pill, hormonal patches and implants may have reduced effectiveness and are less advisable; likewise the combined pill, although it can sometimes be prescribed at increased dose; a copper IUD is the most effective emergency contraception, but if this is not acceptable, levonorgestrel at an increased dose may be effective.

Further information and up-to-date advice should always be sought from specialist services if there is uncertainty.

2. Fertility and assisted conception

Some couples with one partner infected with HIV will want to start a family. If it is the woman who has HIV infection, she can establish when she is ovulating using ovulation kits, and then artificially inseminate using semen from her partner. Many successful pregnancies have resulted from this technique. This method is completely safe for the male partner. Unprotected sex is clearly not recommended, but if a couple choose this, then timing intercourse with ovulation will reduce the exposure and risk to the male partner.

If the man has HIV infection, donor insemination is an option. For conception using the infected partner's sperm, the safest technique is one called 'sperm washing'. This is not considered 100 per cent safe, but no transmissions have been documented. Further information should be sought from the HIV specialist if a couple are interested. Sperm washing is not currently provided at NHS expense. A couple can also choose unprotected sexual intercourse which is timed to reduce the frequency of exposure to HIV (and thus the risk).

Sub-fertility should be addressed in the usual way, although HIV status should be made clear if the couple is referred.

3. Antenatal and postnatal care

Some patients with HIV may be well and actively choose pregnancy. Some may have an unplanned pregnancy that they choose to continue. Some may have undergone the traumatic experience of discovering through antenatal HIV testing that they are infected with HIV.

Managing the pregnancy of a woman with HIV is strongly influenced by the need to prevent transmission to the baby. The risk of transmission can be reduced from around 20 per cent to under 1 per cent by the interventions given on page 19.

Support of bottle feeding

There is evidence that breastfeeding doubles the risk of HIV transmission, and mothers with HIV are advised to bottle feed. This message may not be accepted by all – for some groups breastfeeding has deep symbolic meaning. Unfortunately, the choices in such circumstances are stark, and advice and support should be available from midwives and others involved in care.

GPs are able to prescribe formula feed if they feel it is appropriate.

Asylum seekers

Asylum seekers identified as HIV positive (commonly through antenatal screening) face particular financial difficulties. Amended asylum support regulations allow a payment to be made to women and children who are being supported by the National Asylum Support Service (NASS) to help towards the cost of infant formula for children up to three. Pregnant women who are being supported by the NASS can receive £3 a week assistance towards the cost of milk for the duration of their pregnancy.

Managing HIV-related problems
The GP's role

In many ways, looking after someone with HIV is no different from looking after those with other chronic conditions. The specialist centres are responsible for initiating and monitoring antiretroviral therapies (ART), and remain responsible for prescribing ART. The role of the GP may vary a great deal depending upon the health of the patient. In addition, the relationship the GP has with the patient, and the relationship between the patient and their specialist team, will affect how the patient uses primary care. For many health problems, all that is needed is advice, reassurance or simple treatment. Nevertheless, there are times when immediate referral

For further information on networks and pathways of care, see MedFASH (2003) *Recommended standards for NHS HIV services.*

for assessment is more likely to be appropriate.

It is important for GPs to have active communication with specialist HIV clinics. They should expect to be written to regularly, and should be prepared to notify specialists in return if there are significant changes in the patient's management or circumstances.

Health problems

Physical problems caused by HIV infection are significantly less common in the diagnosed patient now that ART is widely used. A patient with HIV who presents with symptoms might have:

- problems which relate to HIV disease (check the most recent CD4 count)
- side effects of ART
- an unconnected problem.

You may be able to take the first steps to distinguish which of these is the case. A recent CD4 count that is comfortably above 200 makes HIV-related problems less likely. Check which antiretrovirals the patient is on, and check for side effects in the BNF section 5.3 and on page 74.

For side-effects of ART see p58-62

Conditions that require urgent referral

Serious conditions due to HIV disease affect patients with CD4 counts below 200 cells/μL (except TB, see page 29). Symptoms that require careful assessment include:

- respiratory
- visual (even if apparently minor, such as floaters)
- progressive or acute neurological problems.

For more information see pages 27-31.

Side effects of ART are sometimes serious or even life-threatening – check which medication the patient is on.

For serious conditions associated with HIV see p27-31

Commoner conditions

Many HIV-related problems are also common in patients who do not have HIV for example, shingles and seborrhoeic dermatitis. Management of such conditions is generally the same, and the GP is likely to be familiar with treatments. However, the immunosuppressed patient may require longer treatment than other patients.

For guidance on management of commoner individual conditions, see 'Quick reference' page 75.

For managing commoner conditions see p75-78

Caring for people on antiretroviral therapy (ART)

ART has had an enormous impact on morbidity and mortality from HIV disease – in those countries which have been able to afford the drugs. New drugs and strategies are continually being developed. Your patient (particularly if recently infected) has a good chance of living with their HIV for decades.

How the drugs act

For a list of drugs and their groups see p74

Anti-HIV drugs are classified in groups according to where they act in the replication cycle of the virus.

Reverse transcriptase inhibitors

These drugs act on the enzyme (reverse transcriptase) that is key to transcribing the viral RNA into proviral DNA. They are divided into:
- nucleoside (and nucleotide) reverse transcriptase inhibitors (NRTIs)
- non-nucleoside reverse transcriptase inhibitors (NNRTIs)
  There are only two NNRTIs in regular use at the time of writing – efavirenz and nevirapine.

Protease inhibitors

Viral protease is needed as newly formed virus buds from infected cells.

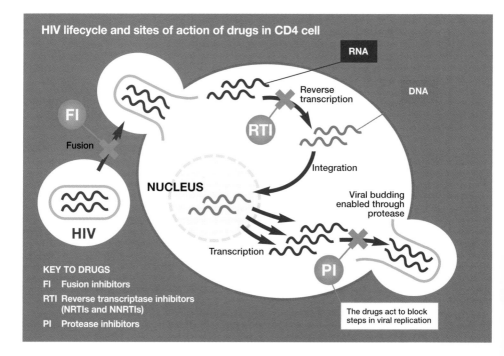

HIV lifecycle and sites of action of drugs in CD4 cell

RNA

Reverse transcription

DNA

FI

Fusion

RTI

NUCLEUS

Integration

Viral budding enabled through protease

HIV

Transcription

PI

KEY TO DRUGS

FI   Fusion inhibitors

RTI Reverse transcriptase inhibitors
     (NRTIs and NNRTIs)

PI   Protease inhibitors

The drugs act to block steps in viral replication

A decrease in production of protease means release of immature virus particles.

Fusion inhibitors
These drugs prevent the viral membrane of HIV fusing with the cell membrane.

Resistance
HIV readily mutates in the process of replication. This means that resistance to single anti-HIV drugs develops very readily. For this reason these drugs are used together in combinations of three or more.

Drug combinations used in ART
For initial regimens, the usual combination is of two NRTIs with one NNRTI. The choice of regimen will depend upon the need to minimise side effects and long-term toxicity, while providing an effective combination likely to suppress the virus long-term and be convenient for the patient. Some people may be taking two NRTIs and one or two protease inhibitors (PIs) while other patients may be taking drugs from several classes. Sometimes tablets containing more than one drug are given in order to aid adherence.

When to start antiretrovirals
HIV specialists will take into account a number of factors when deciding when to start ART, including the CD4 count and risk of disease progression. The choice of drugs will be informed by:

- knowledge of effectiveness of combination
- likelihood of resistance developing to chosen drug
- transmitted drug resistance (the patient was infected by a strain of virus already showing resistance due to past exposure to drugs)
- drug toxicity
- pill burden
- drug-drug interactions.

The indications for commencing treatment and the recommended regimens have changed over time. National guidelines are regularly updated.

See British HIV Association (2003) *Guidelines for the treatment of HIV-infected adults with antiretroviral therapy*, at www.bhiva.org

Adherence to ART regimens

important!

Adherence is essential to prevent drug resistance developing

Resistance of the virus to ART is minimised if combination therapy is maintained at therapeutic levels in the blood stream. Any interference with their action (for example, through drug interactions) or with their administration (for example, through not adhering to prescribed regimens) can lead to resistance developing. Drug resistance, once established, is irreversible. Cross-resistance between classes of drugs means treatment choices are further limited.

If people with hypertension miss out their medication for a short period of time, it will still be effective when they re-start. Unfortunately this is not the case with antiretroviral therapy. Adherence to a long-term drug regimen is one of the biggest challenges to those who live with HIV as well as to those who support them. The timing of the medication through the day may be complex – for example, a patient might be on one drug that must be taken some time before meals, but another that must be taken directly after. Even without these practical complications, it is hard to sustain a regular regimen without losing motivation or even simply forgetting doses.

> Adherence to a long-term drug regimen is one of the biggest challenges to those who live with HIV as well as to those who support them.

Monitoring adherence is something the primary care team can do well. When patients are seen, the GP or practice nurse should assess and monitor how they are coping with taking their medication and whether they are missing doses. Patients need to understand the reasons behind the requirement for optimal adherence as well as the possible consequences of missed doses. If they discontinue or repeatedly miss doses, try to explore the reasons for this. In some areas HIV specialists can arrange adherence support.

Monitoring progress

Monitoring of ART is primarily by viral load (see page 16). The aim is to reduce the viral load to <50 copies/ml (current limit to detection) by three to six months.

Drug interactions

PIs and NNRTIs are the groups most affected by drug interactions, being metabolised via the cytochrome P450 enzyme system in the liver. These interactions can lead to both increased toxicity and decreased efficacy. Dietary substances, herbal remedies and recreational drugs can all interact significantly.

> Check for drug interactions on: www.hiv-druginteractions.org

For further information see: www.hiv-druginteractions.org. Please note that on this site the interaction charts currently list only interactions for PIs and NNRTIs. Interactions for NRTIs with drugs other than the PIs and NNRTIs are not listed. This site includes dietary substances (under herbals/nutraceuticals) and recreational drugs (under illicit/recreational).

In some areas advice from specialist pharmacists is available.

ART side effects

While the benefits of ART are enormous, side effects are common and some are very serious. Even if the patient is not too unwell at presentation, many conditions will progress if ART is continued. However, as antiretrovirals should not be stopped without good reason, management should virtually always be discussed with a specialist before action is taken. An exception to this would be a clinical emergency when advice cannot be obtained.

> Check for side effects on: www.bnf.org, section 5.3

It may take some time for a drug regimen to be found that suits the patient. Because some drugs have significant side effects at first, treatment centres tend to monitor patients more closely for the first six to eight weeks of therapy.

For a full list of both serious and minor side effects, see the BNF section 5.3. See 'Quick Reference' page 74 to identify which group each drug is in.

Minor side effects

ART can cause a huge range of minor side effects, which are generally listed in the BNF. Be careful that minor symptoms do not herald a major side effect – check the major side-effects list below. GPs will often be able to manage minor side effects in the normal way. However, they should always check for drug interactions (see page 58). Symptomatic treatment is given on pages 75-78 (a guide to managing HIV-related problems).

To identify which group a drug is in see p74

Serious or unusual side effects

Side effects are considered unusual when they are peculiar to ART. In other words, they are not the type of problem that GPs would normally consider could be due to medication. In addition, some serious 'unusual' side effects of ART can present in an insidious way, leaving the GP at risk of overlooking their significance.

Serious or unusual side effects of NRTIs
Hypersensitivity

- Abacavir – usually within first six weeks, but not exclusively. Can be life-threatening. Typically causes fever or rash, but may cause a range of non specific symptoms such as fever, vomiting or myalgia. Seek advice urgently if suspected.

Lactic acidosis and hepatomegaly

- Probably caused by all NRTIs.
- This potentially life threatening problem may present with non-specific symptoms such as nausea or loss of appetite. In clear-cut cases patients will be obviously unwell – acidotic, with hepatomegaly, deranged liver function and raised serum lactate. They may have abdominal pain. Such patients need hospital admission and all ART medications are usually stopped. However, some patients are relatively well with a slightly raised lactate and simply need closer monitoring by their specialist. These patients may continue on ART.

Bone marrow suppression (anaemia, neutropenia)

- Most commonly zidovudine, but also lamivudine and stavudine.

Pancreatitis

- Most commonly didanosine, but also stavudine, zalcitabine, abacavir, and lamivudine.
- Specialists will monitor amylase in patients on these drugs.

Peripheral neuropathy

- Mainly with didanosine and stavudine, less commonly lamivudine and zalcitabine. (The latter is rarely used.)
- Management of neuropathic pain generally consists of either tricyclic agents or anti-convulsants such as sodium valproate or gabapentin. Acupuncture can also be very helpful for some patients. Anaesthetic neuropathies are more difficult to manage and significant functional disability sometimes results.

Lipoatrophy

- This is possibly associated with all NRTIs. Stavudine is considered the most implicated, and is currently not recommended as first line therapy.
- This is subcutaneous fat loss that can be one component of lipodystrophy (explained in more detail below – see PIs). It may be associated with hyperlipidaemia and/or diabetes (see PIs below).

Serious or unusual side effects of NNRTIs

Hypersensitivity

- Nevirapine
- Usually within the first four weeks, but not exclusively. Can be life-threatening. Typically causes rash and Stevens Johnson-type syndrome.

Hepatic toxicity

- Nevirapine
- Very rare. May be fatal.

Psychiatric problems

- Efavirenz
- Nightmares, sleep disturbances, mood changes, behaviour changes. Vivid (life-like) dreams commonly.

Serious or unusual side effects of PIs

Hepatic toxicity

- All PIs

important!

Hyperlipidaemia may be associated with lipodystrophy (see page 61), but can also occur in patients on ART who do not have obvious lipodystrophy.

Hyperlipidaemia

- All PIs (and possibly NRTIs) apart from possibly atazanavir.
- ART can raise cholesterol and triglyceride levels – sometimes to an alarming degree. Diet can control levels in some, but those with high levels are increasingly treated with statins (Atorvastatin, Pravastatin) and fibrates (Bezafibrate). Care must be taken when selecting such drugs due to interactions and hepatic metabolism. It still remains unclear if hyperlipidaemia will lead to a rise in cardiovascular disease. However, it seems wise to pay attention to other traditional CVD risk factors such as hypertension and smoking.

For drugs by drug group see p74

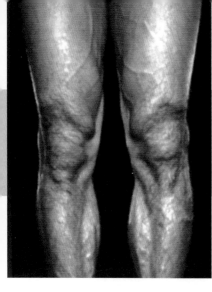

Lipodystrophy.
One of the biggest fears of patients taking ART, this syndrome may also be associated with metabolic abnormalities such as diabetes and hyperlipidaemia.

Lipodystrophy

- First described with PIs, but may be associated with most antiretrovirals. At the time of writing, it is unclear to which drugs it can definitely be attributed.
- Lipodystophy is a syndrome probably caused by ART in which there are changes in the distribution of body fat. In some individuals this is characterised by subcutaneous fat loss causing facial (particularly cheek and temple) thinning and limb and buttock wasting, sometimes known as 'lipoatrophy'. It is particularly associated with NRTIs. Some patients develop central (truncal) adiposity with an increase in intra-abdominal fat, buffalo hump and breast enlargement. This was initially associated with PIs. These two forms of lipodystrophy often co-exist and may also be associated with other metabolic abnormalities such as diabetes (due to insulin resistance) and hyperlipidaemia.
- Lipodystrophy may be one of the biggest fears of patients taking antiretroviral combinations. It can be stigmatising and distressing, in some cases resulting in low self-esteem and depression. Awareness of the possibility of lipodystrophy may be a reason for some patients avoiding medication, and for some it may significantly affect adherence. Treatment for this syndrome is still largely unsatisfactory. A number of specialist centres offer treatment with polylactic acid, a filling agent for facial wasting.

Diabetes (type 2)

- All PIs
- Susceptibility to diabetes – probably through insulin resistance – is associated with PI therapy. This can be managed in the usual way, but monitoring and additional medication may induce 'adherence fatigue' in some patients. This can impact on both HIV and diabetes. Again, it is important to pay attention to other CVD risk factors in such patients. Diabetes may be associated with lipodystrophy (see above), but can also occur in patients on ART who do not have obvious lipodystrophy.

Ureteric colic, nephrolithiasis

- Indinavir

Side effects of fusion inhibitors

As the newest class of antiretrovirals, there is limited knowledge of their side effects at the time of writing. Currently they are given subcutaneously and it appears that most side effects relate to injection sites. However, there is some concern about a form of pneumonitis that may be associated with this therapy.

Additional treatments for those with immunosuppression
Immunotherapy

This term covers a variety of techniques aiming to promote a patient's immunity. Progress has been limited for this therapeutic approach thus far.

Prophylaxis against opportunistic infections (OIs)
Pneumocystis pneumonia (PCP)

For more information on PCP see p28

- Patients who either have a CD4 count of less than 200 cells/μL or have already had an episode of PCP will be offered prophylaxis.
- Co-trimoxazole is the most effective agent, although some patients may use dapsone and some use nebulised pentamidine.
- If the immune system recovers sufficiently following antiretroviral medication, this prophylaxis may be discontinued once the CD4 count is above 200 cells/μL.
- Co-trimoxazole also protects against toxoplasmosis.

Mycobacterium avium intracellulare

- Patients with a CD4 count of less than 50 cells/μL may be offered primary prophylaxis – usually azithromycin or rifabutin.

The patient who will not attend for specialist care

Some patients with HIV drift out of or reject specialist care. If the GP has managed to keep a continuing relationship with the patient, this can be quite a stressful situation. The patient may not respond to discussion about the benefits of specialist care (with or without ART) and the need to attend. The GP should:

useful info

Frequently – given time – the patient will agree to be reviewed at the hospital, or agree to be referred to a different specialist centre.

- try to maintain their relationship with and contact with the patient. This is sometimes the most they can achieve for some time
- explore exactly what the patient's reasons are for not wishing to attend the HIV clinic. There may be a problem that can be addressed. In some areas there is more than one local HIV clinic to which the patient could be referred
- continue to give gentle reminders to the patient of the health benefits of specialist care – whilst trying not to jeopardise the GP-patient relationship
- consider arranging (after discussion with the patient and the local lab) a CD4 count to assess how damaged their immunity is. With a high CD4 count the GP can be a bit more relaxed with the patient about the need for hospital review.

case history

The dangers of being unaware of a patient's HIV treatment

Mr M, aged 38, visited his GP with severe unilateral headaches which had been present for three days. His previous migraine attacks had responded to simple analgesics, but this time they had little effect. He did not inform his GP that he was taking combination antiretroviral drugs (including ritonavir) as he did not think it relevant. The GP prescribed ergotamine by suppository. Mr M later died from an acute myocardial infarction. In this example, the action of the ergotamine was significantly enhanced by the ritonavir inhibiting liver metabolism.

Mr M later died from an acute myocardial infarction.

The dying patient

At the time of writing, the advent of ART has meant that death as result of HIV infection has become much less common. Nevertheless, deaths still occur and the primary care team is likely to be involved in decisions regarding care as death approaches. With ART it is harder to define when a patient is terminally ill, because, given time, there can be recovery of immunity following changes in choice of antiretroviral. However, the patient remains vulnerable to overwhelming infection until that happens. With this uncertainty about outcome, there is a need to integrate palliative and curative approaches to care, and the goals of HIV palliative care need to be redefined.

Planning care and advance directives

Several life-threatening episodes may occur before the final terminal event. So, if not already addressed, planning should begin early on after immunity has started to deteriorate.

People with HIV commonly want to be in control of their care and treatment. All should be helped, if necessary, to express their requirements and preferences, which may change depending on the type of illness or stage of the condition. The desire for maximum patient choice in matters of care and treatment is nowhere more important than during episodes of acute, potentially life-threatening illness or when the patient is clearly approaching the terminal phase. Wherever possible, dying patients should be able to have partner, family, friends and people they trust around them, as well as appropriate medical, nursing and social care.

A well-planned death can also help those left behind to cope with their loss. In the UK, living wills or advance directives were largely developed by and for people with AIDS, though they are now used more widely. GPs may be asked to look at such documents, or contribute to their contents. In such circumstances it is always advisable to seek further

Advance statements about medical treatment – code of practice, report of the British Medical Association, April 1995, second edition due in 2004, available at www.bma.org.uk/ap.nsf/Content/codeofpractice

advice and guidance, for example the BMA's ethical guidance. Copies of an advance directive form can be obtained from the Terrence Higgins Trust. (See page 82 for contact details.)

Involvement of other healthcare professionals

Although the course of advanced HIV disease may be more 'up and down' than other conditions requiring palliative care, GPs should still be able to draw on their experience. Continuity and communication are extremely important in palliative care, and general practice is well-suited to providing these. The patient should be offered the support and involvement of palliative services and community nursing if appropriate. Some GPs can harness the support of specialist community nurses in HIV care. Hospice care may be needed. Respite care and symptom-control are currently the most important indications for admission.

Wills

People with deteriorating immunity should be advised to make a will as a matter of priority to avoid distressing disagreements and resentment after death. For example, at the time of writing same-sex relationships have no legal recognition and long-term partners can be excluded from a share in the estate. Legislation has been proposed in the UK to provide full legal recognition for gay partners.

Death certification

Although a doctor's general ethical duty of confidentiality to the patient continues beyond his or her death, such ethical obligations are generally overridden where there is a statutory duty to disclose. This is made clear by GMC confidentiality guidance which points out that the law requires doctors to complete death certificates honestly and fully. This can be problematic since death certificates are public documents, and surviving partners or family members may fear the consequences if full details are disclosed; or the patient may not have wished their family to know about their HIV infection. Nevertheless, where HIV infection or AIDS is the cause of death, this must be stated, whatever the views of the patient and/or family.

Until recently in cases of HIV-related deaths, doctors have stated the obvious cause of death – for example, bronchopneumonia – but ensured that the box on the back of the certificate is ticked so that further information can be given at a later date. This has been crucial for the accuracy of national and regional statistical information. Increasingly, however, there is demand for very clear and robust mortality data and at the time of writing it is unclear whether or how this will affect HIV reporting on death certificates in the future.

SECTION 4

HIV and the practice team

HIV and the practice team

There is a place for HIV prevention in the daily activities of the primary care team.
Practice policies and systems can help to ensure that the patient with HIV receives high quality care and staff are adequately prepared to provide this.

Sexual health promotion and HIV prevention in the practice

Growing concerns about the deterioration of sexual health in the UK is leading some practices to consider how they might play a part in promoting sexual health and reducing HIV transmission. For this role, clinical workers in primary care need both factual information and skills in sexual history taking and risk assessment.

For more information on this see *Handbook of sexual health in primary care* to be published by fpa in 2005.

Practice nurses and GPs have opportunities to:
- discuss and assess risk of having or acquiring HIV with individual patients
- promote safer sexual practices and condom use with those who are or may be at risk
- promote HIV testing when appropriate
- promote hepatitis B testing and immunisation when appropriate
- support harm minimisation with injecting drug users.

Sexual health promotion interventions may occur during:
- travel advice consultations
- new patient checks
- contraceptive care
- cervical screening.

Working with those with diverse needs

HIV can affect and infect anyone, but in the UK it is still most common in certain population groups:
- men who have sex with men
- people from countries in Africa, especially south of the Sahara
- injecting drug users.

Members of all these groups may already feel marginalised or stigmatised in UK society, and this can be exacerbated by the stigma and discrimination associated with HIV. Practitioners in primary healthcare need to be aware of some of the emotional and social pressures on these groups.

Men who have sex with men

This term is used to include both men who identify as homosexual (and may call themselves 'gay') and those who have sexual encounters with other men without considering themselves to be homosexual. Gay men may have a sense of belonging and access to gay-oriented culture. However, other men who have sex with men may see themselves as bisexual or even heterosexual, are sometimes married, and may not be open about their same-sex encounters.

African communities

Fear and prejudice against HIV is often very high in African communities, with resultant stigma and secrecy. Many people from very high prevalence countries will know of family members or friends who have had, or died from, HIV. HIV may affect both parents as well as their children (infected or not), creating major family needs. HIV information and safer sex advice, presented in a culturally sensitive way, is essential in this group. The GP's knowledge of the local community also helps in providing a focus of care for families affected by HIV and AIDS.

Injecting drug users

Those who have acquired HIV through injecting drugs (even if they no longer use drugs) may be aware of a double stigma – as drug users they are a socially excluded group, and this may be compounded by their HIV status. Those who have not wished, or been unable, to access support may be locked in a cycle of problems as they try to fund and feed their drug use. Dependent drug use may restrict the ability to attend appointments or take medication regularly. In some, HIV may quite simply not be a priority in the face of the daily problems associated with drug dependence.

For more information see the *Substance misuse management in general practice* website, www.smmgp.demon.co.uk

GPs involved in appropriate substitute prescribing in primary care will be aware of the benefits of this for the patient, in terms of harm reduction and access to healthcare.

Practice policies and systems

Ensuring confidentiality and avoiding discrimination

Developing a practice that is alive to patient concerns about confidentiality and fears of discrimination is likely to support:

- open discussion of, and testing for, HIV with those who may be at risk
- open discussion about safer sexual and injecting practices
- improved quality of care for people with HIV infection.

Some patients perceive negative attitudes towards them from some GPs and health centres. Many also have fears relating to confidentiality, especially around sensitive information such as HIV status, sexual orientation or lifestyle. Several studies have shown that the following interventions help in allaying the fears of patients:

- ensure that your practitioners and clinicians are non-judgmental and empathic to different lifestyles. Consider in-house training for the team
- develop and implement a non-discrimination policy with your practice – then display it to your patients
- develop and implement an appropriate confidentiality statement – then display it to your patients.

Systems and record keeping
To support HIV testing

For pro forma record sheet see p73

There are different systems which may be used to support HIV testing in the practice:

- a pro forma record sheet or computer template can be used to collect data on individual patients having an HIV test. The contents of a pro forma should be discussed and agreed with clinical team members – there is a potential that highly confidential information of little value to future care may be unnecessarily recorded. However, if items are excluded for this reason then a check list or aide-memoire may be needed:

For aide memoire see p72

- an aide-memoire (computer or paper-based) may help ensure that all issues are covered. It does not record individual patient information.

For the patient with HIV

Some patients infected with HIV will be anxious about how their HIV status is to be recorded in the practice. It is best to raise the subject so this issue can be addressed and the benefits outlined (as well as the risks if the diagnosis is not clearly recorded).

- **Coding HIV infection**
  Computer systems may have different ways – or different options – for coding HIV infection. Computer screens should not be visible to third parties, although this may be difficult to achieve in a small consulting room. If screens are visible to patients, the visibility of what is recorded should be considered, noting the fact that the patient may be accompanied, but not consulting for an HIV-related problem. The practice will need to be able to search for patients with HIV infection in order, for example, to invite them for flu immunisation or to invite women for annual smears.
- **Records to support clinical care**
  The success of practice systems depends on reliable and rapid communication from the hospital each time the patient has attended and also when significant test results become available.
- **Records of antiretroviral and other drugs**
  Even if drugs are prescribed solely by the hospital, a clear record should be kept. On some practice computer systems it is possible to keep a

record of drugs prescribed 'outside', which is the safest option as long as each and every hospital letter is checked for medication changes.

- **Records of CD4 count and viral load**
  Computer systems may enable a simple template to be set up for use with patients with HIV. The most recent blood results can then be entered when they are made available by the hospital.

- **Review date**
  A review date system can act as a reminder to check that records are up to date. It is better to spend time chasing an absent CD4 result before you are faced with a patient with a bad cough.

Health and safety

Hepatitis B immunisation

The practice should have a system to ensure that all staff who handle clinical specimens are immune to hepatitis B.

Prevention of needle stick injuries

Universal precautions in handling sharp instruments and body fluids are essential to reduce the risk of contracting HIV or other blood-borne viral infections in the healthcare setting. Approved sterilisation procedures and adequate disposal of sharp instruments are crucial components of this process. It is easy to forget the number of undiagnosed blood-borne infections, so it is essential to assume that all patients are potentially infected.

> **important!**
>
> A 'high risk' needle stick injury requires rapid and decisive action. Ensure all team members are aware of the practice policy on PEP.

Management of needle stick injuries

A 'high risk' needle stick injury requires rapid and decisive action if post exposure prophylaxis (PEP) is to be given in time. Discuss, develop and implement a practice policy on PEP and ensure all team members are aware of its existence and whereabouts.

For PEP see p19

PEP policies in primary care should:

- advise how to manage the wound
  - make clear the urgency and limited window of opportunity
  - make clear who should be contacted for advice in your locality and how
  - take into account other blood-borne viruses such as hepatitis B and C
  - be adopted only in association with discussion and training.

> Further information to support development of your policy can be found in *HIV post-exposure prophylaxis: guidance from the UK Chief Medical Officers' Expert Advisory Group on AIDS (2004)*, available at www.dh.gov.uk, or obtained from local infection control or occupational health specialists.

The HIV-infected healthcare worker

The majority of procedures carried out in the primary care

setting (assuming appropriate infection control procedures) pose no risk of transmission of HIV from healthcare worker to patient. Employing people infected with HIV is generally not a risk except in certain very specific situations where patients' tissues might be exposed to a carer's blood following injury ('exposure prone procedures').

However, the Department of Health requires all healthcare workers who are infected with HIV to seek appropriate expert medical and occupational health advice, and this should include (where relevant) how to modify or limit their work practices to avoid exposure prone procedures. HIV-infected healthcare workers must not rely on their own assessment of the risk they pose to patients.

While protecting the health and safety of our patients, we must at the same time respect the right to confidentiality of our staff and colleagues. Employers should assure infected healthcare workers that their status and rights as employees will be safeguarded so far as is practicable.

See Department of Health (2002) *Guidance on the management of infected health care workers and patient notification* available at www.dh.gov.uk

SECTION 5

Quick reference

IN THIS SECTION

Quick reference

Checklists and sources of further information for doctors and patients

HIV testing aide-memoire

Does the patient understand:
- how HIV is transmitted
- the difference between HIV and AIDS
- the medical advantage of knowing HIV status
- that the test is for antibodies, not the virus itself
- the significance of the three-month window period and the possible need for a repeat test?

Discussion of risk
- risk to date
- future risk / risk reduction

Discussion of implications of positive test

Confidentiality

Coping with the wait
- Who knows you are having the test?
- Who is it safe to tell?

Ask the patient not to drink alcohol or take drugs on day of result

Other useful questions
- Is there any written information that should be given to the patient?
- Is the test best done in primary care?
- Should there be any associated tests?
- Are any repeat tests required to cover the window period?
- Has the patient given clear consent to HIV (or other) tests?
- Check their contact details
- Have you arranged an appointment for the result to be given to patient?
- Does the patient have a supply of appropriate condoms/lubricant?

HIV testing pro forma

HIV TEST REQUEST **CONFIDENTIAL** Date _____

Patient _____ DOB ———————————

Reason for test
☐ patient request ☐ investigation of illness ☐ needlestick ☐ insurance ☐ travel ☐ antenatal
☐ doctor concerned ☐ other:_____
If patient request, reason for test:
Other issues (eg depression, relationship problems, worries about sexual orientation, drug use)

Assessment of risk
Risk behaviours:

Timing of risk (especially within 3 months):
Patient's understanding of risks:

Understanding
☐ Nature of HIV test   ☐ 3-month window period   ☐ Natural history of HIV

☐ Monitoring and treatment   ☐ Confidentiality   ☐ Life insurance

☐ Safer sex   ☐ Safer injecting   ☐ Pregnancy

☐ Other_____
Screen for:

HEPATITIS A	☐ Yes ☐ No		HEPATITIS B	☐ Yes ☐ No	
HEPATITIS C	☐ Yes ☐ No		CHLAMYDIA	☐ Yes ☐ No	

Coping, help and support
Is this the right time for a test? What would be the worst thing if the result was positive?
Who will you tell? Who do you not have to tell?

The HIV test
In window period   ☐ Yes ☐ No   Advise to repeat test ☐ Yes ☐ No
Appointment for result _____   Will be accompanied? ☐ Yes ☐ No

Support whilst awaiting result (GP, family, friend, telephone helpline)
_____
_____
_____

Reproduced with the permission of the Royal College of General Practitioners Sex, Drugs and HIV Task Group and the Primary Care Facilitation Team (Blood Borne Viruses), NHS Lothian.

Antiretrovirals by group

This list was correct at the time of writing. Up-to-date lists of agents are available on the following websites: www.bhiva.org, www.bnf.org, and www.hiv-druginteractions.org

Current antiretroviral drugs

Nucleoside/tide reverse transcriptase inhibitors (NRTIs)		Protease inhibitors (PIs)	Non-nucleoside reverse transcriptase inhibitors (NNRTIs)	Fusion inhibitors
abacavir	(1592)	amprenavir/fosamprenavir	efavirenz	enfuvirtide T-20
didanosine	(ddl)	atazanavir	nevirapine	
emtricitabine	(FTC)	indinavir		
lamivudine	(3TC)	lopinavir		
stavudine	(d4T)	nelfinavir		
tenofovir		ritonavir		
zalcitabine	(ddC)	saquinavir		
zidovudine	(AZT)	tipranavir		

Trade names

- These are not often used for single drug tablets.
- Trade names of combination tablets are used more commonly and are listed opposite.
- Trade names are all given in the BNF.

Tablets containing more than one drug

Trade name	Contains
Combivir	lamivudine, zidovudine
Kaletra	lopinavir, ritonavir
Trizivir	abacavir, lamivudine, zidovudine

Drug interactions – further information

Either

- Check which ART class or group the antiretrovirals in question belong to (see table above or BNF).
- Then check www.hiv-druginteractions.org;

Or

- Use the most recent BNF.

A guide to managing HIV-related problems

A patient with HIV who presents with symptoms might have:
- problems which relate to HIV disease (check the most recent CD4 count)
- side effects of ART
- an unconnected problem.

With oral medication beware of interactions with antiretroviral therapy, see www.hiv-druginteractions.org.

Constitutional symptoms

Condition	Notes	Management
Night sweats	Exclude serious causes	Little helps: supportive management only
Fatigue	Exclude serious causes	Approach as for palliative care.
Weight loss	Test for low testosterone in men	High calorie supplements.
Anorexia	TFTs in all	Testosterone replacement sometimes used if deficiency confirmed, seek specialist advice.

Skin conditions

Condition	Notes	Management
Fungal infections		Generally respond to topical antifungals. Prolonged or repeated treatment may be required.
Herpes zoster Herpes simplex		Will respond to antivirals such as aciclovir but longer courses at higher doses may be needed. Long term use of antivirals is helpful if the problem is recurrent.
Warts Molluscum contagiosum		Cryotherapy.
Bacterial infections eg impetigo folliculitis		Topical antibiotics. Oral antibiotics needed more commonly than in patients with intact immunity.
Seborrhoeic dermatitis		Topical anti-fungal and hydrocortisone combinations. Anti-fungal shampoos may be helpful.
Psoriasis		Usual management, but may be much less responsive.
Kaposi's sarcoma		Will require specialist treatment.

SECTION 5

The mouth

Condition	Notes	Management
Oral candida	Can cause significant discomfort and difficulty in eating/drinking	Topical or systemic anti-fungal agents (nystatin, fluconazole). Long term use of antifungals occasionally indicated if the problem is recurrent.
Aphthous ulceration		Topical oral steroid creams.
Oral hairy leukoplakia		Sometimes improved by a course of aciclovir (but oral hairy leukoplakia is usually asymptomatic and does not require treatment).
Gingivitis	Maintaining good oral hygiene and dental care is important for all immunocompromised patients	Chlorhexidine mouth washes. Oral metronidazole. Referral to dentist.
Kaposi's sarcoma		Requires specialist treatment. May disappear with ART.
Dental abscess		Oral antibiotics. Referral to dentist.

The rest of the gastrointestinal tract

Condition	Notes	Management
Nausea	May be caused by ART	Managed with either a dopaminergic agent (metoclopramide or domperidone or more commonly haloperidol with its longer half life) or agents such as levomepromazine.
Oesophageal candida		As for oral candida (see The mouth above).
Diarrhoea	Possible causes: • HIV in the intestinal mucosa • intestinal pathogens • side effect of ART Take stool samples	Loperamide for symptomatic treatment. Codeine is sometimes helpful. Salmonella and campylobacter can be more severe and difficult to treat. Less common organisms such as cryptosporidium sp and microsporidium sp may be responsible. Management should be guided by culture results and information on drug interactions: seek specialist advice if necessary.

Respiratory problems

Condition	Notes	Management
Chest infection	Exclude PCP see pages 27-28 Exclude TB-like infections see page 29	'Ordinary' chest infections will respond to the usual antibiotics such as amoxicillin.

Neurological problems

See also page 30 for serious conditions that require admission

Condition	Notes	Management
Peripheral neuropathy	May be caused by HIV or ART	Pain management similar to usual approaches to neuropathic pain. Gabapentin or other drugs used in neuralgia may help.

Genital problems

Condition	Notes	Management
Genital candidiasis		Topical or systemic anti-fungal agents (clotrimazole, fluconazole). Systemic antifungals are sometimes used long term to prevent recurrence.
Genital herpes		Aciclovir – may be needed in longer courses and at a higher end of the dose range than usual. Long-term use of aciclovir or similar may be used to suppress frequent recurrences.
Genital and perianal warts		Frequently recurrent and more difficult to treat. Topical therapy (podophyllotoxin or imiquimod) or cryotherapy may help. Refer to GUM clinic unless responding well to topical therapy.

Sexual dysfunction

Condition	Notes	Management
Erectile dysfunction Loss of libido	May be multifactorial. HIV related causes include: • effect of HIV • fear of transmitting infection • ART • vascular problems In men check testosterone level	Sildenafil and tadalafil can be used, but they interact with PIs and NNRTIs and expert advice should be sought. Testosterone replacement is sometimes used on specialist advice.

Psychiatric problems

Condition	Notes	Management
Stress	Stress is common May be exacerbated by stigma	Supportive counselling and/or specialist or psychological support is sometimes necessary.
Depression Bipolar disorder	May be seen more commonly in people with HIV Some antiretrovirals may be associated with psychiatric disturbance	Beware drug interactions if considering antidepressants.
HIV-related brain impairment	Can cause functional impairment and lead to significant care needs	Seek specialist advice. Consider needs of carer(s).

Visual problems

See page 30 for CMV retinitis, a serious condition that requires urgent referral to ophthalmology.

Useful sources for clinicians

Organisations and websites
aidsmap
www.aidsmap.com
A wealth of information on HIV and ART, including updates on the latest research findings.

Drug interactions
www.hiv-druginteractions.org

Epidemiology: Health Protection Agency
www.hpa.org.uk
Up-to-date figures for HIV and other infections in the UK, including graphs and slides that can be downloaded and *CDR Weekly*, an electronic epidemiological bulletin.

British HIV Association
www.bhiva.org
Regularly updated guidelines for treatment of HIV-infected adults with ART, and associated guidelines (HIV in pregnancy, HIV and hepatitis co-infection, adherence support). Also hosts website of Children's HIV Association (CHIVA) containing articles and protocols on treatment and care of HIV-infected children.

Substance misuse management in general practice
www.smmgp.demon.co.uk
Organisation to give information and support to GPs prescribing for drug users. Produces a regular newsletter.

Royal College of General Practitioners sex, drugs and HIV task group
www.rcgp.org.uk
The task group produces a six-monthly update. Information on the group is found by clicking on 'groups and forums' then 'Clinical and Special Projects Network'.

British Association for Sexual Health and HIV
www.bashh.org
Professional organisation that produces clinical effectiveness guidelines for the management of STIs.

Useful reference documents to have in the practice

- Association of British Insurers & British Medical Association (2002) *Medical information and insurance. Joint guidelines from the British Medical Association and the Association of British Insurers*. London: British Medical Association. (Available at www.bma.org.uk)

- Department of Health (1996) *Immunisation against infectious disease*. London: HMSO. (*The Green Book* – available at www.dh.gov.uk with new chapters and updates)

- Carter Y, Weyman A, Moss C and Belfield T (eds). *Handbook of sexual health in primary care*. London: fpa. For publication in 2005.

- General Medical Council (2004) *Confidentiality: protecting and providing information*. London: General Medical Council. (Available at www.gmc-uk.org)

- Rogstad et al (2004). HIV testing for patients attending general medical services: concise guidelines. *Clinical Medicine* **4**:136-9.

- UK Health Departments (2004) *HIV post-exposure prophylaxis: guidance from the UK Chief Medical Officers' Expert Advisory Group on AIDS*. London: Department of Health. (Available at www.dh.gov.uk)

Useful sources for patients

Leaflets to have in the practice

- *HIV.* fpa, (2004).
  An information leaflet about HIV and HIV testing for the general public.
  Available free of charge in England through the DH Publications
  Orderline, PO Box 777, London SE1 6XH. Tel: 08701 555 455.
  Fax: 01623 724524. Email: dh@prolog.uk.com
  Available in the rest of the UK from fpa direct (01685 846678) at £5.00
  per 50 copies.

- *Tell me about HIV. Your questions answered.* UK Coalition of People
  Living with HIV and AIDS (2004).
  For those who have just been diagnosed with HIV.
  Available from UK Coalition of People Living with HIV.
  Tel: 020 7564 2180 or email: info@ukcoalition.org for the attention of
  John Clarkson, Distribution Manager.

- *Anti-HIV Drugs.* National AIDS Manual (2003),
  Basic information for people with HIV about antiretroviral drugs. Deals
  briefly with dosing, side effects, drug interactions and drug resistance.
  Available from National AIDS Manual (NAM) – see details below.

Other written resources for people with HIV

- NAM patient information series (currently 10 booklets)
  Plain English information on key treatment topics.
  For organisations 50p each, minimum order £10.
  Order by phone (020 7840 0050), fax (020 7735 5351) or online
  (http://aidsmap.com/bookshop/order_form.asp)
  Available free for people personally affected by HIV (email
  info@nam.org.uk).
  Electronic versions can be downloaded from the NAM website
  (http://www.aidsmap.com/publications/infoseries/index.asp)

- Terrence Higgins Trust (THT) *Living Well* leaflet series
  Information to enable people living with HIV to remain well informed and
  positive about life.
  Prices vary according to booklet and quantity ordered. For more
  information see http://www.tht.org.uk/publications/pubs_liv.htm

- *Positive Nation*, the UK's HIV and sexual health magazine, published by
  the UKC (UK Coalition of People Living with HIV and AIDS). Free to
  anyone living with HIV. For subscription details see
  http://www.ukcoalition.org/PositiveNation/subscriptions.html

Organisations for support and information

You may well have local organisations working with people with HIV. Here we list just a few national organisations, which may give you the means of identifying local ones.

Terrence Higgins Trust (THT)

www.tht.org.uk

A large charitable organisation with services in many British towns and cities. Produces a wide range of written resources on HIV prevention and living with HIV and runs the THT Direct helpline (0845 1221 200). For an advance directive form (see pages 63-64) phone the helpline.

National AIDS Manual (NAM)

www.aidsmap.com

Extensive online information on treatments and research. Database of HIV organisations worldwide (including UK). Some online information resources available in French, Portuguese and Spanish. Also publishes comprehensive HIV reference collection, *The NAM Manual*.

National sexual health helpline

0800 567 123

24-hour, free, confidential helpline for anyone concerned about HIV or sexual health. Can provide details of local HIV organisations.

Waverley Care

www.waverleycare.org

Charity providing support services and information in Scotland. (Information centre: 0131 661 0982).

THT Cymru

www.tht.org.uk/regions/tht_cymru

Regional branch of Terrence Higgins Trust, providing support services and information in Wales. (Helpline: 0800 074 3445).

The HIV Support Centre

www.thehivsupportcentre.org.uk

Provides support services and information in Northern Ireland, including a helpline (0800 137 437).

Bibliography

- Adler MW (ed) *ABC of AIDS*. London: BMJ Publishing Group.

- Association of British Insurers and British Medical Association (2002) *Medical information and insurance. Joint guidelines from the British Medical Association and the Association of British Insurers*. London: British Medical Association. (Available at www.bma.org.uk)

- BHIVA Writing Committee on behalf of the BHIVA Executive Committee (2003) British HIV Association (BHIVA) guidelines for the treatment of HIV-infected adults with antiretroviral therapy. *HIV Medicine* **4** (suppl 1): 1-41. (Available at www.bhiva.org)

- British Medical Association and Association of British Insurers (2003) *GP insurance package*. London: British Medical Association. (Available at www.bma.org.uk)

- British Medical Association (1995) *Advance statements about medical treatment – code of practice, report of the British Medical Association*. 2nd edition due in 2004. (Available at www.bma.org.uk)

- British Medical Association and Royal Pharmaceutical Society of Great Britain. *British National Formulary* (BNF). (New edition every six months – available at www.bnf.org)

- Carter Y, Weyman A, Moss C and Belfield T (eds). *Handbook of sexual health in primary care*. London: fpa. For publication in 2005.

- Department of Health (1996) *Immunisation against infectious disease*. London: HMSO. (*The Green Book* – available at www.dh.gov.uk with new chapters and updates)

- Department of Health (2001) *Oral sex and transmission of HIV – statement of risk* (Available at www.dh.gov.uk)

- Department of Health (2003) *Screening for infectious diseases in pregnancy: standards to support the UK antenatal screening programme*. London: Department of Health. (Available at www.dh.gov.uk)

- General Medical Council (2004) *Confidentiality: protecting and providing information*. London: General Medical Council. (Available at www.gmc-uk.org)

SECTION 5

- Lyall EG, Blott M & de Ruiter A et al (2001) British HIV Association. Guidelines for the management of HIV infection in pregnant women and the prevention of mother-to-child transmission. *HIV Medicine* **2**: 314-34. (Full version available at www.bhiva.org)

- Medical Foundation for AIDS and Sexual Health (2003) *Recommended standards for NHS HIV services*. London: Medical Foundation for AIDS & Sexual Health. (Available at www.medfash.org.uk)

- Rogstad et al (2004). HIV testing for patients attending general medical services: concise guidelines. *Clinical Medicine* **4**:136-9.

- UK Health Departments (2002) *AIDS/HIV infected health care workers: guidance on the management of infected health care workers and patient notification*. A consultation paper. (Replaces the 1998 guidance. Available at www.dh.gov.uk)

- UK Health Departments (2004) *HIV post-exposure prophylaxis: guidance from the UK Chief Medical Officers' Expert Advisory Group on AIDS*. London: Department of Health. (Available at www.dh.gov.uk)

SECTION 6

Subject index

Subject index

Notes: page numbers suffixed by 'f' indicate figures,
those suffixed by 't' indicate tables.

INDEX

G

gabapentin 60, 77
gastrointestinal conditions 35, 76
   see also specific conditions
gay men 50–51, 67
wills 64
genital problems 25, 35, 37, 77
gingivitis 34, 76
GPs, clinical care role 54–55

H

haematological problems 36
health and safety issues, primary care
teams 69–70
healthcare workers, HIV status 69–70
health promotion 19, 51, 66
helper T cells *see* CD4 cells
hepatitis A 52
   immunisation 52
hepatitis B 13, 52, 66, 69
   antenatal screening 19
   immunisation 44, 52
   testing 44, 52
hepatitis C 13, 69
   testing 44
hepatomegaly 59
herpes, genital 35, 77
herpes simplex 33, 75
herpes zoster (shingles) 14, 14f, 25, 33,
55, 75
heterosexually acquired infection 10, 11f
high-risk groups 41–42, 66–67
   identification 42
HIV
   lifecycle 56
   p24 antigen 15
HIV antibody test *see* testing (HIV antibody
test)
homosexuals 50–51, 67
hyperlipidaemia 60

I

immunisation 20, 52–53
Immunisation Against Infectious Disease 52
immunosuppression 25, 27, 62
immunotherapy 62
impetigo 33, 75
indinavir 61, 74
infant feeding 54
infection, primary *see* primary infection
infections
   chest 28, 29, 77
   dental 76
   eyes 30
   frequency 47
   immunisation 52–53
   opportunistic 14, 28-29, 32, 62
   sexually transmitted 13, 35, 51, 66
   skin 33, 75
   see also specific infections
influenza immunisation 52
information sources 72–82
   HIV testing aide-memoire 72
   HIV testing pro forma 73
   organisations and websites 79
   for patients 81–82
injecting drug users 20, 51, 67
insurance reports 40
intra-uterine devices (IUCDs) 53

K

Kaletra 74
Kaposi's sarcoma 14, 33f
   management 75, 76
   oral involvement 34, 35
   respiratory involvement 28
   skin tumours 31, 33

L

lactic acidosis 59
lamivudine 59, 60, 74
libido, loss of 78
lipoatrophy 60, 61
lipodystrophy 18, 60, 61

pro forma 73
   raising the subject 42
results, informing patients 45–46
   screening for HIV 42
systems and record keeping 68–69
thrombocytopaenia 36
thrush (oral) 34, 76
tinea cruris 33
tinea pedis 33
tipranavir 74
toxoplasmosis 62
treatment *see* clinical care
Trizivir 74
tuberculosis (TB) 14, 29, 32, 37
tumours 14, 31, 33, 34
   risk and CD4 counts 15t
   see also specific tumours

Z

zalcitabine 59, 60, 74
zidovudine 59, 74

U

undiagnosed infection (HIV) 12, 13, 40
Unlinked anonymous testing programme 13
unprotected sex *see* sexual practices
ureteric colic 61

V

viral load 16–17, 16f, 69
   antiretroviral monitoring 58
viral skin infections 33, 75
virus (HIV) *see* HIV
visual problems 30, 55

W

warts 33, 35, 75, 77
websites, information sources 79
wills, dying patients 64

Y

yellow fever immunisation 52